"Arise, Sir Knight!"

©2020 Catherine Fet · North Landing Books · All Rights Reserved

Why are the Middle Ages *middle*? The middle of what?

In the history of Europe, the **Middle Ages** – or the **medieval period** – are the time between ancient history, which ends with the fall of the Roman Empire in the 5th century, and the history of the modern world, which starts with the European **Renaissance** in the 15th century. However, the period between the 5th and 10th centuries is often called the **Dark Ages**, or the **Early Middle Ages**. Many of the things we associate with the Middle Ages, such as castles, knights, crusades, and Gothic cathedrals, appeared in the 11th century. The period between the 11th and 15th centuries is often called the **High Middle Ages**.

In the Dark Ages, after the Roman Empire fell apart and Rome was sacked by barbarians – tribes from the north – many achievements of the Roman, Greek, and other ancient civilizations were lost. The territory of the Roman Empire was split between many local warlords. Borders disappeared and warrior migrants plundered whatever remained of the ancient cities, farms, and ports. There were neither laws, nor governments. The roads were dangerous and no longer maintained. The structures that had brought water to the fields fell apart. Trade between different lands nearly stopped. Education nearly disappeared. Arts and literature nearly died.

 # KING ARTHUR

Many scholars believe that King Arthur, a legendary British warrior, was one of the kings of the Dark Ages. However, the legends about King Arthur come from later sources, starting with ***Historia Regum Britanniae** – **The History of British Kings*** – written in Latin, in 1138, by Geoffrey of Monmouth. Geoffrey of Monmouth presents Arthur as a Dark Ages king who lived in the last decades of the Roman Empire. He tells stories of King Arthur's battles against Saxons and Romans, as well as against monsters, witches, and giants. He also mentions King Arthur's advisor, the wizard Merlin, and his wife Queen Guinevere. In Geoffrey of Monmouth's book, King Arthur successfully grows his kingdom and defeats the Roman Empire.

"King Arthur" by Charles Ernest Butler

As his army is marching toward Rome, Arthur hears that his nephew Mordred, whom he left to rule Britain, has seized the throne and married Arthur's wife Guinevere! Arthur returns to Britain and defeats Mordred, but he is wounded. Taken to the island of Avalon to be healed Arthur is never seen again. Geoffrey of Monmouth, writing hundreds of years later, says that even though so many centuries have passed, King Arthur is still alive, and will one day return from Avalon and rule Britain again!

Geoffrey of Monmouth's *History of British Kings* became so popular that many more collections of tales about Arthur and his court appeared in the 12th and 13th centuries. The new legends focused on the **Knights of the Round Table**. Traditionally, at a royal feast, the king would sit at the head of a rectangular table, with the most important guests next to him. But the legends of King Arthur say that at his court in the Kingdom of Camelot he and his knights sat at a round table, showing that all the knights were equals.

One of the most important legends about the knights of the Round Table is the legend of the **Holy Grail**. ***Perceval, the Story of the Grail*** written in 1190 by the French poet Chrétien de Troyes, tells the story of Perceval, one of the knights of the Round Table. One day Perceval meets the Fisher King, fishing in a boat on the river. The king invites Perceval to stay at his castle. At dinner, Perceval sees a mysterious procession pass through the Fisher King's hall: First comes a man carrying a spear dripping blood, then two kids carrying candelabras, then a young girl carrying a richly decorated grail, or cup, followed by a lady carrying a silver plate. Seeing this, Perceval says nothing, and never asks about the grail. That was a mistake, because Perceval would have learned that

"Perceval sees the Holy Grail" by A. Spiess

the grail was a holy object with mysterious healing power. Chrétien de Troyes' poem was not finished, and it never explained what was in the ***grail*** cup. Later legends said that it was the cup of communion that Jesus offered to his disciples – the apostles – the night before he was captured by his enemies. Legends also said that the blood of Jesus was collected in that cup when he was dying on the cross.

More and more stories appeared about the grail – the **Holy Grail**. In these stories the knights of the Round Table traveled all over the world looking for the Holy Grail. In modern English, the words **holy grail** are often used to describe a goal that is hard to reach. Another legendary object in the tales of King Arthur is his sword *Excalibur*. *The Death of Arthur*, written by the 15th-century English writer Thomas Malory, says that Excalibur was given to King Arthur by the Lady of the Lake, a water fairy. As Arthur was crossing the lake in a boat, her hand appeared from the water holding the sword. When King Arthur was wounded, he asked one of his knights to take Excalibur and throw it back into the lake. But the knight was enchanted by the beauty of the sword and decided to keep it. When he came back to Arthur, the king asked him, "What did you see when you threw the sword into the lake?" "Nothing but ripples," said the knight, and Arthur knew he was lying. Finally the knight threw the sword into the lake, and he saw the hand appear from under the water and take it. Then a boat appeared on the lake. There were three queens in the boat, all wearing black hoods. King Arthur asked his knights to put him on that boat. The boat then left, never to be seen again.

"The death of King Arthur" by James Archer

CHARLEMAGNE
748 – 814

"Charlemagne" by Albrecht Dürer

Charlemagne is often called the *Father of Europe*. He was the first leader since the fall of Rome to unite much of Western Europe under one banner. *Charlemagne* (shar-le-main), or *Charles le Magne* is French for *Charles the Great.* Charlemagne was the king of the Franks. The Franks were a Germanic people who lived in the territory of modern-day Western Europe. The Frankish kings had unified many tribes, and adopted Christianity from the Roman Empire.

In the early Middle Ages, a number of Germanic tribes, such as the Goths, Huns, Franks, and Saxons, struggled for power in Europe. Also, there was a new threat from outside Europe – Muslim (Islamic) invaders from the Middle East and North Africa. Byzantium, the Eastern portion of the Roman Empire, with its capital in Constantinople, fought off the Muslim invaders in the East, but in Western Europe Germanic tribes were the only force that could stop an Islamic conquest.

Charlemagne was named Charles after his grandfather, Charles Martel, or *Charles the Hammer*. Charles Martel won the famous Battle of Tours against the armies of the Umayyad Empire, temporarily stopping the Islamic invasion. But when 26-year-old Charlemagne became king, he faced the same forces – the Saxons and other Germanic tribes attacking the Franks in Europe, and Muslim armies pushing into Europe from the south.

Charlemagne was very successful both as a ruler and a warlord. He grew his kingdom for 40 years until it spread over the territory of present-day France, Germany, Belgium and The Netherlands.

In 800 a revolt broke out in Rome against Pope Leo III. During a celebration, when Pope Leo was greeting a procession of chanting Christians, the conspirators attacked him. They tried to blind him and attempted to cut out his tongue! Fortunately, they failed, but Leo was badly wounded. He escaped from Rome, crossed the Alps mountains into Charlemagne's lands, and asked Charlemagne for protection.

"The coronation of Charlemagne" by Friedrich August von Kaulbach

Charlemagne went to Rome with his army, restored Pope Leo to power, and ordered the conspirators executed. But Pope Leo pointed out that Jesus Christ instructed Christians to forgive their enemies, so instead of execution the conspirators were sent into exile. While in Rome, on Christmas Day, Charlemagne went to the Church of St. Peter, and as he knelt before the altar, the Pope put a gold crown on his head, saying: "Long live Charles Augustus, Emperor of the Romans."

It was the first time the title *emperor* was used in Rome since the fall of the Roman Empire. Charlemagne's kingdom became the **Holy Roman Empire**. Interestingly, Charlemagne's court historian Einhard writes that Charlemagne had no idea that Pope Leo was planning to crown him Roman Emperor. It was a surprise! Charlemagne realized that he was crowned emperor only after the crown was placed on his head!

What kind of a person was Charlemagne? Einhard writes: "Charles was tall and strong, his eyes very large and expressive, nose a little long, hair fair, and face laughing and merry. Although his neck was thick and short, and his belly rather large, this didn't spoil his appearance... He wore simple linen shirts and pants, an otter fur coat in winter, and a blue cloak. He always carried a sword – usually one with a gold or silver hilt and belt."

A denarius of Charlemagne with the inscription 'Karolus Imperator Augustus,' AD 812

Ninth-century poet and historian Notker the Stammerer writes that Charlemagne often wore an outfit made of a simple white sheepskin, something poor people would wear in those days. But his friends and military commanders loved expensive clothes. Once Charlemagne decided to teach them a lesson and surprised them with an invitation to go hunting with him. They didn't have time to change, and followed him wearing fancy clothes of silk and fine leather decorated with feathers of pheasants and peacocks, purple and lemon-colored ribbons and precious ermine fur. After a day of hunting those amazing clothes "were torn by branches of trees, thorns, and briars, drenched with rain and covered with the blood of wild beasts." They were completely destroyed. But Charlemagne had his sheepskin washed and it looked like new!

"At meals Charles listened to reading or music," writes Einhard. "The subjects of the readings were the stories and deeds of olden times... " Charlemagne learned and spoke foreign languages, such as Latin and Greek. He took lessons in public speaking, philosophy, and especially loved astronomy... It sounds like Charlemagne was an educated man, but the truth was exactly the opposite. He had received no education in his youth. "He also tried to write," adds Einhard, "and kept blank writing tablets in bed under his pillow, so that he could practice drawing the shapes of letters any time. However, since he started learning to write only late in life, he had no success at this at all." That's right, Charlemagne was illiterate! He learned everything by ear, since he didn't know how to read or write.

Charlemagne had 18 sons and daughters, although many of them died early. He loved his kids, says Einhard. "He never ate without them when he was at home, and never made a journey without them." He invited Alcuin, the famous English poet and scholar, to teach him and his kids. Charlemagne insisted that not only children from noble families, but also the children of the poor should go to school. One of his orders reads, "Let every monastery and every abbey have its school, where boys may be taught music, singing, arithmetic, and grammar, and let the books which are given them be free from mistakes, and let care be taken that the boys do not spoil them when reading or writing." When he returned from one of his campaigns, he sent for a group of schoolboys and asked them to show him their work. He noticed that the children of the poor showed more knowledge than the children of the rich. It is said that he scolded lazy kids from noble families saying: "You think only of your dress and play. You think your family wealth will help you out. Wrong: If you waste time when you are young you will be good for nothing when you grow up."

Joyeuse ('joyful' in French), a sword that is said to have belonged to Charlemagne

Early in his reign Charlemagne demanded that the people of the cities and the tribes he conquered become Christians or face death. Alcuin, however, explained to him that this was against the teaching of Christ. "Faith is a free act of the will, " he said. "You can force people to be baptized, but you cannot force them to believe." Charlemagne agreed with him, and in 797 he abolished the death penalty for being non-Christian.

"He was a very friendly man," writes Einhard about Charlemagne. "Not only did he make friends easily, but he was loyal to them and appreciated their friendships." Despite many battles with the Muslim Arab invaders whom Europeans called *the Saracens*, Charlemagne managed to create ties of friendship with the legendary Caliph Harun al-Rashid who ruled the Abassid Islamic empire from Baghdad in present-day Iraq. Charlemagne had a dream. He wanted... an elephant!
He asked Harun al-Rashid if Harun could help him get one. Harun had such respect for Charlemagne, says Einhard, that he sent him his own elephant, named Abul-Abbas, which was the only elephant he owned!

In 799 Charlemagne sent ambassadors carrying precious gifts to Harun al-Rashid asking him to allow Christians to visit the Holy Land, the land of ancient Israel, that was under Harun al-Rashid's rule. Among the gifts were German hunting dogs. "They were of remarkable swiftness and fierceness," writes Notker the Stammerer.

"Charlemagne cuts down the sacred 'Irminsul' pillar which the Saxons had worshipped before they became Christians" by Hermann Wislicenus

"Harun Al Rashid receives gifts from Charlemagne" by Julius Köckert

Harun decided to test the dogs and ordered Charlemagne's ambassadors to take the dogs on a lion hunt. "When they came in sight of the lion," continues Notker, "Harun's advisor said to the Franks: 'Now set your dogs on to the lion.' The German dogs caught the lion, and the Frankish ambassadors killed it with swords of northern metal...At this sight Haroun said, 'Now I know that what I heard of my brother Charles is true – that by the frequent practice of hunting, and by constant training of his body and mind, he has learned to conquer anything that is beneath the heavens.'" He announced that he would give the Holy Land to Charlemagne: "I will give that land into his power; and I will rule over it as his representative."

As the ambassadors were leaving Harun's court, he sent with them a few gifts for Charlemagne. Harun was much wealthier than the king of the Franks, and his gifts were things unheard of in Europe. They included horses, silk clothes, perfumes, and a chess set made of ivory! Among the gifts was also a water clock. Each hour a bronze ball dropped into a bowl of water and mechanical knights – a different one for each hour – appeared from little doors which then shut behind them! Nobody in Europe had ever seen such a precious object. Charlemagne and his friends thought it was magic! Charlemagne died in 814 and his empire fell apart.

A talisman that is said to have belonged to Charlemagne

ALFRED THE GREAT
849 – 899

The Life of King Alfred, composed in Latin in 893 by Asser, the Bishop of Sherborne, opens with these words: "In the year of our Lord 849 was born Alfred, king of the Anglo-Saxons, at the royal village of Wanating in Berkshire, which country has its name from the forest of Berroc, where boxwood grows most abundantly." Alfred was the son of Ethelwulf, king of the West Saxons, who spent most of his life defending England from the Vikings, the Norse people from Scandinavia, who plundered all lands they could reach by sea. In Old English the name Ethelwulf means *Noble Wolf*, and Alfred means *Elf Wisdom*.

"One day, when Alfred was a child," writes Asser, "Alfred's mother showed him and his brother a Saxon book of poetry, and said, "I will give this book to one of you – the one who will learn to read it first." Alfred rushed to take lessons in reading, and studied hard all week. He proved the best reader and his mother gave him the book. King Alfred often complained, says Asser, that when he was young there had been few teachers in his land, and he hadn't received a good education, and when he grew up and became king, "there was no time for reading." But all his life and "even until his death, he continued to feel the same insatiable desire for knowledge, and sought more and more learning."

When Alfred became king he was 23 years old. Around that time the Vikings started raiding England more and more often. The Vikings were Norwegian and Danish pirates, especially active during the so-called *Viking Age*, the 9th to 11th centuries.

"The boyhood of King Alfred" by Edmund Blair Leighton

"Viking sea battle" by Otto Ludvig Sinding

The Anglo-Saxons were Christians. Christianity had come to Britain in the 1st century, probably brought by Roman soldiers. The Vikings believed in their own Norse gods, such as **Odin** – the god of war, **Thor** – the god of thunder, **Loki** – the god of mischief, and **Freya** – the goddess of love. Some of the Viking gods' names are preserved in the English names of the days of the week! Tuesday = **Tyr's Day**, Wednesday = **Odin's day**, Thursday = **Thor's day**, Friday = **Freya's day**. The English viewed the Vikings as **pagan** (non-Christian) barbarians seeking to destroy Christian faith and culture.

By the time of Alfred's reign most of northern and eastern England had already been seized by the Danish Vikings. Viking ships were swift, with a single sail and up to 20 rowers. Vikings were skilled and ruthless warriors. They didn't hesitate to sail up the large rivers deep inland and capture whole towns. To protect his kingdom, Alfred decided to take his line of defense to the sea, and built the first English navy. In 875 he gained the first naval victory ever won by England. But since the Vikings already held a huge chunk of England, they had an advantage. More and more of them came from the north pouring into Alfred's lands. Defeated, Alfred had to flee for his life and hide. For months he wandered through forests and marshes, and slept in caves, all alone. He worked for shepherds and farmers to get food. One day a pig farmer gave Alfred shelter. The farmer's wife was baking cakes, says Asser, while the king, sitting by the fireplace, made ready his bow and arrows. Suddenly the farmer's wife noticed that the cakes were burning and scolded Alfred. "Couldn't you watch the cakes," she screamed at him, "Don't you see them burn? I bet you are fast enough when it comes to eating them!" "The woman had no idea it was king Alfred," says Asser, "who had fought so many battles, and gained so many victories."

Bishop Asser thought King Alfred had been defeated because his people didn't fully support him. "In the beginning of his reign, when he was a youth, he would not listen when his people asked him for help or justice," Asser wrote. Now Alfred was 30 years old. God taught him a lesson so "he might learn that there is one Lord to whom every knee bows, and in whose hand are the hearts of kings – the Lord God who throws down the mighty from their seat and raises the humble."

A legend says that while hiding from the Vikings, Alfred disguised himself as a wandering singer, or **minstrel**, and went into the camp of the Danes. He played harp and sang Saxon ballads. The Vikings liked his singing so much, they brought him to their leader, the warlord Guthrum. Guthrum loved the songs and gave food and gifts to the minstrel. Alfred left, having collected a lot of information about the enemy troops. "The same year, after Easter, King Alfred with a few followers made for himself a stronghold in a place called Athelney," continues Asser. From this fort Alfred started rebuilding his army and preparing to attack the Danish invaders. His first big victory was at the Battle of Edington in 878 where King Alfred's army defeated the Viking army led by Guthrum. Guthrum and Alfred made a treaty that divided England between the Anglo-Saxons and the Vikings. They made an old road running across England from London to Chester the border between the two kingdoms. In that agreement Guthrum also promised that he would become a Christian.

Left: pages from the Anglo-Saxon manuscript – the Gospel of Matthew, in Latin, with an illustration showing Matthew, the gospel-writer. The book was created in the middle of the 8th century. In the 9th century it was looted by Vikings, and the English had to pay the Vikings to get it back.
Below: "King Alfred disguised as a minstrel" by Daniel Maclise

"King Alfred at the baptism of Guthrum" by Andrew Benjamin Donaldson

The legends describe the first meeting between Guthrum and Alfred after Guthrum's defeat. "Were you that wandering minstrel?" asked Guthrum. "Yes," replied Alfred, "I was the minstrel to whom you were so generous. Your life is now in my hands, but I will give you freedom if you will become a Christian and never again make war on my people." The Viking king kept his word. Three weeks after the agreement was made, he came to King Alfred and was baptized. In baptism he was given a new name, Ethelstan, which means **Noble Stone**.

King Alfred believed that his victories would not have been possible without his faith and the wisdom he gained from Christianity. He ordered his court scholars to start translating Christian books from Latin to English, and decreed that schools should teach kids not in Latin, but in English, their native language.

London was on the border between Alfred's kingdom and the lands held by the Vikings. In 886, Alfred started rebuilding London within the old walls built by the ancient Romans who had founded the city of Londinium. Alfred put his son Ethelred in charge of creating a new street plan and a set of new walls for London. Meanwhile Guthrum died, and a number of power-hungry Viking warlords tried to capture his kingdom. The Viking attacks on Alfred's lands began all over again! A Danish navy of 330 ships arrived at the English shores.
The Vikings brought their wives and kids:
They had no plans to return to Scandinavia.

Gold Saxon belt buckle, AD 600

"Viking ships on the river Thames" by Everhardus Koster

Despite their numbers, Alfred's army defeated the Danes. Retreating, the Vikings sailed up the River Thames and made themselves a fortress north of London. Alfred ordered his ships to block the river and cut the Vikings off from the ocean. Outsmarted, the Vikings ran and many of them left England for good. King Alfred divided his army in two. While one group would stay home with their families, the other guarded the borders against Viking raids.

King Alfred is the only English ruler to be called *the Great*. His wife, Ealhswith, was called "the true and dear lady of the English" by medieval English historians. The name *Ealhswith* means **Hall of Strength**. Alfred and Ealhswith had five children. Their oldest son, Edward, became king after Alfred's death.

A Viking-Age helmet and a Viking ship

"Norwegian Vikings land in Iceland" by Oscar Wergeland

ERIK THE RED  950 – 1003

Erik Thorvaldsson, known as Erik the Red, was a Viking explorer. They say that he was called **Red** because of the color of his hair and beard. Eric's life and adventures are described in ***The Saga of Erik the Red*** composed around AD 1200. Sagas were collections of histories and legends created in Iceland in the Middle Ages.

10th-century silver Viking pendant 'Thor's Hammer'

Erik the Red was born in Norway in 950. His name, Erik, or ***Eirìkr*** in the Old Norse language, means ***Eternal Ruler***. When he was 10 his family moved to Iceland. When Erik was 32 he lived on a farm. One day his slaves accidentally caused a landslide that destroyed his neighbor's farm. The neighbor killed the slaves. Erik killed the neighbor. A Viking judge sentenced Erik to exile and forced him to leave Iceland for 3 years. Erik married his girlfriend, Thjodhild, and moved to an island nearby. But soon he got into another fight that ended in the death of his enemy, and the court made him an ***outlaw*** for 3 years. In Viking times an outlaw was a person whom the law would no longer protect. So if anyone wanted to kill an outlaw for revenge, it was ok.

Erik was scared and decided to go where his enemies couldn't find him. If you climb Snaefell, Iceland's tallest mountain, you can see a huge island on the horizon. Erik sailed there. His ship turned around the southern tip of the island, later named Cape Farewell, and sailed up the western coast. Eric came ashore on a narrow strip of land – the only area that wasn't covered with year-round ice. "During the summer he proceeded into the unpeopled districts in the west, and was there a long time, giving names to the places far and wide," says **The Saga of Erik the Red**. He called the island **Greenland**. Why? Because "men will desire much more to go there if the land has a good name."

For 3 years Erik lived there hunting narwhals, the whales that live in the northern seas. Narwhals have a straight spiraling tusk (a long tooth) poking out of their mouth. Vikings sold narwhal tusks in Europe as **sea unicorn horns**. Europeans were crazy about unicorns, and believed that the sea unicorns looked like a horse with a horn who lived under the sea!

After 3 years in Greenland Erik the Red returned to Iceland and was met as a hero explorer. In 985, he took 25 ships to Greenland, but after a terrible storm only 15 ships reached the shore. The Vikings built a town there, and continued the narwhal hunting started by Eric the Red. Erik's village in Greenland lasted until the 15th century, selling the **sea unicorn** horns for 500 years!

The Saga of Erik the Red also tells the story of a famine the Vikings experienced in Greenland: "At that time there was a great famine in Greenland. Those who had been out on fishing expeditions had caught little, and some had not returned." There was a woman in the Viking settlement by the name of Thorbjorg who was a sorceress, a witch. The name Thorbjorg means **Thor's protection** in the Icelandic language. The saga describes the magic ritual performed by Thorbjorg to stop the famine.

Narwhal tusk and ruins of a Viking settlement in Greenland

Thorkell, the settlement chief, invited Thorbjorg to his house. "A high seat was prepared for her, and a cushion laid on that seat was stuffed with soft feathers...Thorbjorg wore a blue cloak decorated with gems, and a necklace of glass beads. Over her hair lay a black hood of sheepskin, lined with ermine fur. A staff in her hand bore a knob inlaid with gems. Her gloves were of ermine fur, white and furry inside... There was prepared for her a porridge made with goat milk, and the hearts of many and different of animals were cooked for her. She had a brass spoon, and a knife with a handle of walrus-tusk mounted with two rings of brass. The point of it was broken off."

The next day Thorbjorg prepared for her magical ritual. Women of the settlement formed a ring. Thorbjorg asked if any of them were familiar with the magic spells known as **weird-songs**. A girl named Gudrid said she knew **weird-songs**, but refused to sing them. "I can't help you with this," she said, "because I am a Christian woman." But Thorbjorg, the witch, answered: "You can help your own people, and you are not going to lose anything, you know." Gudrid agreed to sing. "Then sang Gudrid the weird-song, and it was so beautiful, that no one there had ever heard any song sung in a voice so beautiful before," says **The Saga of Erik the Red**. When Gudrid finished, the witch announced that the ritual was over and that the famine "will last no longer."

Meanwhile, Erik's son, Leif Eriksson, spent some time in Norway with the Viking King Olaf Tryggvason. Olaf had become a Christian, and suggested that Leif bring Christianity to Greenland. Even though Leif's father, Erik the Red, didn't like Christinity and was true to his Viking faith, Leif agreed. He told the king, however, that it wouldn't be easy to change the faith of the Greenland Vikings. "But the king said that he knew no man who was better fitted for the work than Leif," says **The Saga of Erik the Red**. "You will carry with you good luck," said the King. "That can only be if I carry yours with me," replied Leif.

On the way to Greenland Leif's ship was caught in a dangerous storm. Leif lost his way, and ended up sailing toward a new land of which he had never heard before. "There were fields of wild wheat, and vines, and among the trees there were maples..." That was North America! Leif Erikson came ashore near modern-day Newfoundland, Canada in A.D. 1000 – almost 500 years before Columbus, who reached America in 1492.

Narwhal

"Leif Eriksson discovers Vinland" by Christian Krohg

Once home in Greenland, Leif gathered his friends and proposed to go back to the land he had discovered. He asked his father to join them, but Erik's horse stumbled on the way to the harbor, and Erik refused to go, saying "It's a sign of bad luck! I should never discover any other land than Greenland." Leif and his friends sailed West. They came to a shore where tall mountains were covered with snow. This is thought to have been the coast of the modern-day Canadian province of Newfoundland and Labrador. Then they reached a coast that had white sand, rivers full of salmon, and meadows covered with tall grass. In the woods they found grapes! This is thought to have been today's American state of Rhode Island. Leif became the founder of the first European settlement in the Americas. He called the newly-discovered land **Vinland** because of the grape vines found there.

So where did the Vikings go? What happened to them? Vikings lived by conquest, gathering riches by plundering the lands they attacked. They believed that after death you go to the world of the dead where you will need all the things you had when you were alive. When they died, they had all their treasures buried with them, and didn't leave anything to their kids. But when Christianity came to Northern Europe, it brought a different view on death and treasures. Christians believe that the only thing that matters when you die is having lived your life as a good and kind person. Christians didn't bury treasures in their graves. Whatever they had, they left to their kids. As Vikings became Christians, they stopped plundering and amassing treasures, and... stopped being Vikings!

After he had visited North America, Erik's son Leif returned to Greenland where he preached Christianity. Many people became Christians including his mother, who inspired Viking settlers to build the first church in Greenland. Leif Erikson "brought Christianity to the land.. and he was called Leif the Lucky," concludes ***The Saga of Erik the Red***.
And that was the beginning of the end of the Viking times.

Above: "Preaching Christianity to the Saxons" by Albert Bauer

Left: "A Viking funeral" Vikings often buried their dead by putting them on a boat and setting the boat on fire. Sometimes the boat was pushed into the ocean. It burned and sank loaded with the dead Viking's family treasures and animals killed as a sacrifice

A Christian Viking tombstone with inscription in runes. The Runic alphabet was used in Northern Europe from the 1st to 11th centuries.

EDWARD THE CONFESSOR
1003 – 1066

Edward the Confessor takes an oath at his coronation

Edward the Confessor became the king of England in 1042. He was born in England, but his parents, King Ethelred and Emma of Normandy fled to Normandy (part of modern-day northern France) to escape from an invasion of Danish Vikings. Normandy was named after the **Normans**, Vikings from Norway, who had settled along the coast of France. Through a treaty with the King of France, Normandy became a **Duchy of France** and its ruler was called the **Duke of Normandy**.

Edward lived in Normandy until he was 38 years old, when he returned to England to become king. After all those years in Normandy, Edward spoke French better than English, and most of his friends and advisors were Normans.

Edward was more interested in church life than in ruling his land as king. He let his advisors and military commanders rule, while he focused on building churches and monasteries in different parts of England, including Westminster Abbey in London. After his death Edward was named a saint by the Church, with the title of **the Confessor**.

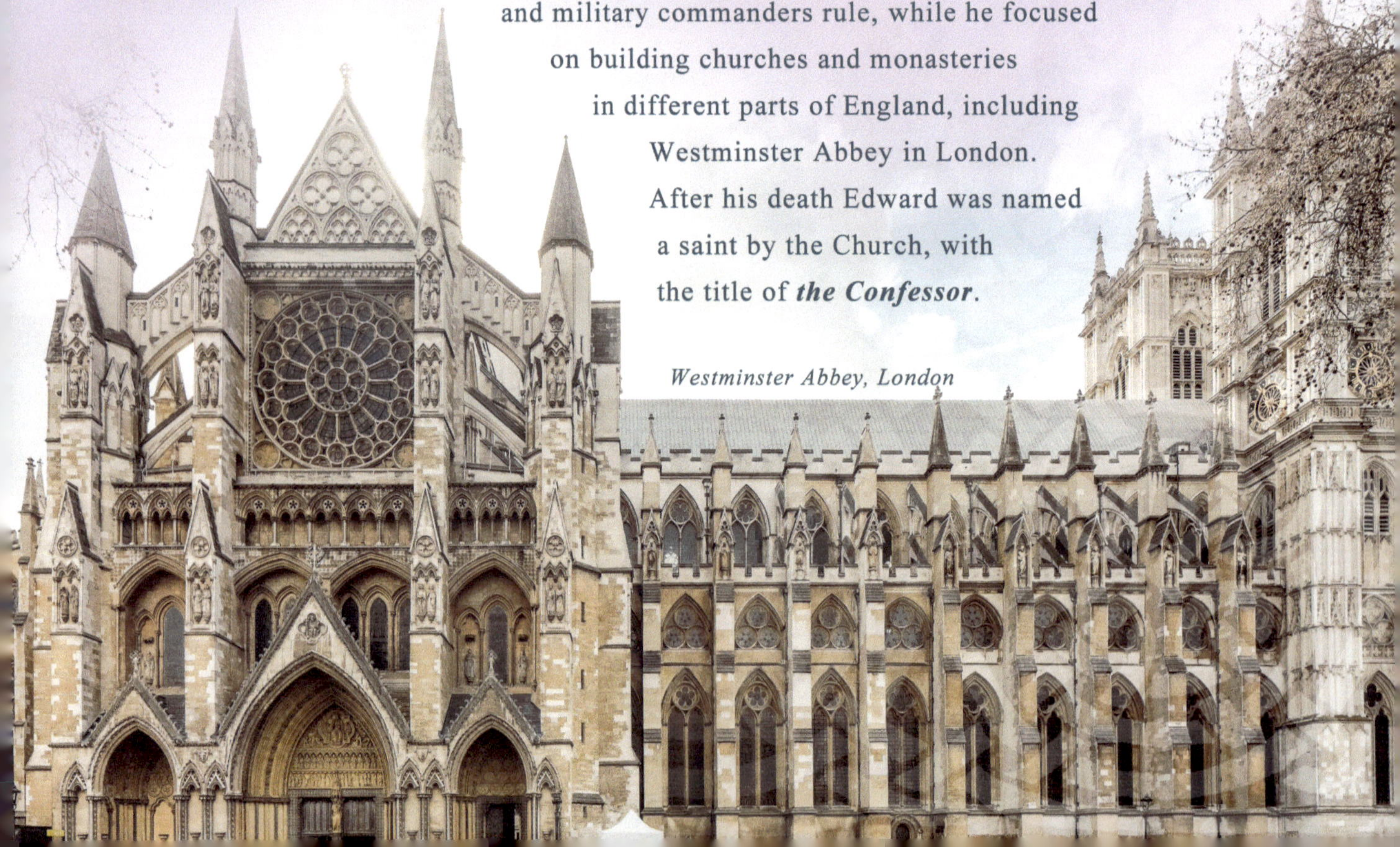

Westminster Abbey, London

One of William Shakespeare's famous plays – *Macbeth* – is set in the time of Edward the Confessor and is based on real events that happened during his reign. A Scottish nobleman named Macbeth invited Duncan, the King of Scotland, to his castle and murdered him. He tried to make it look like the murder had been committed by Duncan's servants. The king's son and heir, Prince Malcolm, had to flee from Scotland, and Macbeth seized the throne – his plan all along! Prince Malcolm asked Edward the Confessor for help. Malcolm wanted a certain number of soldiers to march into Scotland in order to retake the throne.

Edward gave orders to double that number. Leading the English army, Malcolm attacked Macbeth, and after several battles drove him from Scotland and took back the throne.

Edward never had children. Before he died he named his wife's brother, Harold, king. Harold was a good leader, but his reign was short. He lost to a powerful rival, Edward's cousin, William, Duke of Normandy – known to history as William the Conqueror.

In William Shakespeare's play it was Macbeth's wife, Lady Macbeth, who persuaded him to murder King Duncan. Later she lost her mind and wandered around the castle seeking to wash blood off her hands.
Above: "Macbeth and Lady Macbeth" by Robert Smirke
Right: "Lady Macbeth" by Alfred Stevens

WILLIAM THE CONQUEROR

1027–1087

When Edward the Confessor lived in exile in Normandy after a Danish invasion of England, he stayed in the palace of his cousin William, the Duke of Normandy. William treated Edward with kindness and honor, and William expected that in gratitude Edward would make him his heir and pass the English throne to him. William later said that Edward had actually promised he would do that.

One day in 1066 when William was hunting in the woods near Rouen, a messenger came riding toward him shouting "King Edward is dead! And his brother-in-law Harold is the new King!" William called his knights together and said to them, "I will have to take the English throne by force. Will you support me?" The knights agreed to follow him into battle.

Meanwhile, England was attacked by Norwegian Vikings. They claimed the English throne because, before King Edward, England had been ruled by Norwegian King Cnut the Great. Harold, the new King of England, gathered his army, met the Norwegians at Stamford Bridge on September 25, 1066, and won the battle. The Battle of Stamford Bridge is considered by many historians to mark the end of the Viking Age.

Below: "The Battle of Stamford Bridge" by Peter Nicolai Arbo; right: King Harold

While Harold's army was weakened by the clash with the Vikings, William had built 700 warships to carry his army of 10 thousand men to the shores of England. Harold's army was only 7 thousand men. On October 14, 1066 the two armies fought a battle near the town of Hastings in the south of England. William, in full armor, was in the front lines of his troops riding his black war horse sent to him as a gift by the King of Spain. Suddenly a panic broke out among the Norman soldiers: They heard a rumor that William was killed. William of Poitiers who was a chaplain in the household of William the Conqueror, described this moment in his book *The Deeds of William*: "Seeing that his soldiers were running and being chased by the enemy, William rushed toward them, met them as they fled and stopped them, shaking his spear. Baring his head and lifting his helmet, he cried, *Look at me. I am alive, and with God's help I will conquer*." The battle continued from morning till night. Harold fought on foot at the head of his army. Suddenly an arrow shot by one of William's soldiers hit Harold in the eye and killed him. His men gave up the fight. William won the Battle of Hastings.

"The body of King Harold brought to William" by Ford Maddox Brown

From Hastings William marched toward London, burning any towns that didn't surrender. As he approached London, some noblemen and citizens came out to meet William and offered him the English crown. On December 25, 1066, William was crowned in Westminster Abbey by Archbishop Ealdred. As was the custom, the Archbishop asked the noblemen who had gathered for the ceremony, "Will you have William, Duke of Normandy, for your king?" They answered, "We will." At that moment they heard "Fire! Fire!" The buildings surrounding the cathedral were set on fire. There were rumors of revolt. There was bitter hatred for the Normans in England. William didn't even speak English, even though he kept promising he would learn it.

One of the first things William did, was to seize gold and objects of art from the English churches. He needed money to fight wars, put down revolts, and buy the loyalty of the people and the warlords in England and Normandy. "Treasures remarkable for their number and kind and workmanship had been amassed in churches... Of these William generously gave a part to those who had helped him win the battle, and distributed most, and the most valuable, to the poor and to the monasteries of various provinces."

A few months of peace followed. At some point William went to Normandy for a visit, leaving his brother in charge of England. The moment he left a revolt broke out in England. William rushed back and punished the rebellious towns by destroying every single house and farm, causing thousands of people to die from lack of food and shelter. To prevent any secret activity under the cover of the night, he made a law that all lights should be put out and fires covered with ashes at eight o'clock every evening. At 8 PM a bell was rung in all cities and towns throughout England. The bell was called the *curfew*, from the French words *couvre feu*, meaning *cover fire*. In Normandy *curfew* was a way to limit wood- and candle-burning at night and prevent fires, but in England this law was new and seen as a government act of tyranny against the people.

Another thing that made the English angry at William was his ***Doomsday Book***. In order to collect taxes, he sent his men throughout the kingdom to find out just how much property each person owned. His men went into every house, shop and farm, and wrote down who owned what in a special document called the Doomsday Book. ***Doomsday*** means ***the end of the world.*** The document was given this name because its records were supposed to be final. Most of the facts we know about the society and the economy of England in those days come from this document.

The reign of William the Conqueror forever changed the English language. William gave his Norman friends all the important positions in the government and the army, so the English had to learn a lot of French to speak with their new Norman leaders. The old English language was now only for common people in the countryside. To be successful you had to at least mix French words into your English. And at the royal court they spoke only French! Many English words of Germanic origin have a 'fancy' French counterpart that appeared after the Norman invasion: *to light up – to illuminate*... *to ask – to inquire*... *to live – to reside*... *funny – ridiculous*... *to bring – to deliver*... and so on.

To strengthen his hold on England, William ordered the building of many castles and forts – among them the central *keep* of the Tower of London, the White Tower. The castle *keep* was a fortified tower with spiral stairs. Going up, the stairs always turned clockwise to make the right-handed attackers expose more of their body as they fought with swords.

In 1078 King William had a falling-out with his eldest son, Robert Curthose. Curthose was a nickname. It meant *short boots*, and was given to Robert because he was not as tall as his father. In his *Ecclesiastical History* 11th century historian Ordericus Vitalis described Robert as "a talkative, well-spoken, very bold and courageous man with a loud voice." In 1078 Robert asked King William to let him rule Normandy. William refused. Robert joined forces with other young Normans from powerful families, and started an uprising back home in Normandy.

Robert Curthose and the White Tower in The Tower of London

Suddenly King William found out that his wife, Robert's mother, Matilda of Flanders, was secretly supporting Robert. She was sending him advice, information, and money to arm his supporters! When Matilda spent all her money helping her son, she sold her jewels, then her most expensive clothes, then her gold and silver cups and dishes – so she could keep sending money to Robert! William couldn't believe it. He rushed back to Normandy. Imagine the conversation William and Matilda had over this!

William gathered his knights and attacked Robert, but Robert and his friends won the battle against his father! After all he was the son of William the Conqueror! William was wounded in the arm and, to his shame, had to flee the battlefield! At that point Matilda put pressure on her husband and her son to find a compromise. William promised Robert to name him king of Normandy in his will and they made peace.

But then more troubles came. William's son Richard perished while hunting. They said he died at the site of a church burnt by William. They also said that the ghosts of the priests from that church were seen walking around in white robes at night chanting 'There shall be three, there shall be three.' Then William's wife Matilda died. It was a crushing blow: William and Matilda loved each other despite all their disagreements. In the following years disastrous fires destroyed many towns of England. Then came famine and epidemic diseases. And on top of that William started a war with the king of France.

In 1088 William's troops burned the French town of Mantes. The ground where the town had stood was nothing but a bed of glowing embers when William rode over its ruins. His horse stumbled on one of the hot embers. William fell off his horse and was injured. They took him to Rouen, where he lay ill for six weeks... and died. It was said that his servants and even his sons abandoned him in his last hours. All alone, William the Conqueror fell from his bed to the floor, where his body was found many hours later.

Matilda of Flanders

"Death that passes neither rich men nor poor, seized him also," wrote an unknown monk in *The Anglo-Saxon Chronicle*. "He that was before a rich king and lord of many lands, of all his land had now only seven feet of his grave... He used to wear gold and gems, but now he lies covered with mold!"

During William's burial at the church in the town of Caen, a man stepped forward and said that the land on which the church was built belonged to his family. It had been seized by William unlawfully and never paid for. The bishop who performed the funeral service took the man aside and put in his hand money equal to the value of a few square feet - enough for a grave. He promised to pay for the rest of the land after the funeral.

William the Conqueror and Matilda of Flanders had 9 children. After William's death, Robert Curthose became the Duke of Normandy, and his younger brother William became king of England.

"Funeral of William the Conqueror" by Jean-Paul Laurens

EL CID   1043 – 1099

Rodrigo Díaz de Vivar was a warlord in medieval Spain. The Spanish called him *El Campeador* which meant the *Master of the Battlefield* in old Spanish. The Moors – the Muslim Arabs of North Africa – called him *El Cid*, which came from the Arabic *al-sayid* – master. El Cid fought many battles and became the hero of the medieval Spanish epic poem *El Cantar de Mio Cid* – **The Song of My Cid**, or **The Song of the Cid**. Epic poems were long tales used in the ancient and medieval world to preserve and share facts about historical events and legends of heroic deeds.

In the time of El Cid, the Northern half of Spain belonged to the Spanish Christians, while the Southern half belonged to the Moors. The Spanish kingdoms included Castile, Leon, Aragon and others. El Cid lived in Castile.

King Fernando of Castile and the king of Aragon argued about a city each of them claimed. There was a medieval custom that allowed a dispute to be decided by combat. Each side chose a warrior, and the two warriors fought one-on-one. King Fernando chose El Cid. Even though El Cid was very young and the other warrior was much more experienced, El Cid won, and the disputed city became part of Castile. El Cid became famous – but soon his fortunes changed.

When Fernando's son Alfonzo became king, he became angry with El Cid, and in 1081 El Cid was banished from his kingdom. Three hundred of El Cid's knights went into exile with him.

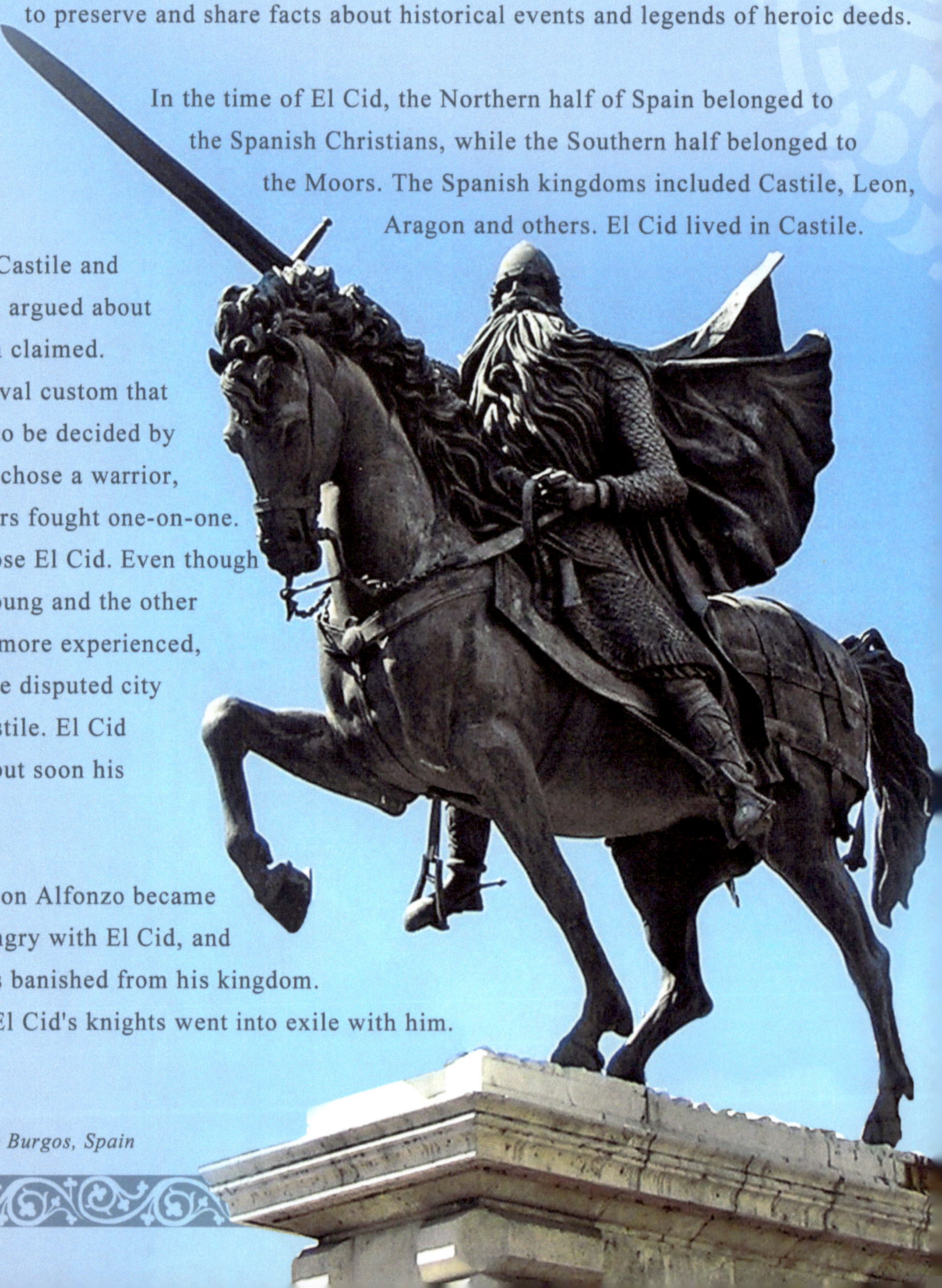

Monument to El Cid in Burgos, Spain

The Song of the Sid says that the king sent out an order saying,

'May no man give shelter to Rodrigo in his need,
And if one gives him shelter, that person may indeed
Lose everything he owns, and also lose his eyes,
So he obeys his lord the King from then until he dies.'
The people felt great sorrow, and from El Cid they hid.
And no one dared to tell the truth to my brave lord, El Cid.
El Cid was looking for an inn, since it was evening late.
But when he came there, he saw that they had barred the gate.

El Cid had no money, so he found two expensive chests covered with red leather and gold, filled them with sand, locked them, and sent them to a couple of wealthy money lenders. He said he would like to borrow six hundred Spanish marks. He would leave the money lenders his treasures of silver and gold packed in two chests, but the chests must not be opened for one full year. The money lenders agreed. El Cid left his wife Ximena and his children at a monastery in Castile. He gave the abbot a hundred marks saying, "I leave my wife and children in your care, and when this money is gone, use your own money to take care of them. For every mark you spend I will give your monastery four."

The Song of the Cid says that while he was leaving Castile El Cid felt certain that there were great battles and victories ahead for him. He was inspired by a mystical vision he had in a dream:

When it was night El Cid lay down. And soon asleep he fell,
And in his dream spoke to him Archangel Gabriel:
"Ride forth, El Cid, Campeador, for never any knight
Has ridden forth under a star whose promise was so bright.
Good fortune will be with you, your star will rise and beam."
El Cid woke up, and crossed himself, remembering his dream.

Above: Castle of Morella, said to have been recaptured from the Moors and rebuilt by El Cid
Right: Statue of Ximena Diaz, wife of El Cid, in Burgos, Spain

A legend says that King Alfonzo was suspected of having murdered his brother Sancho. El Cid made him swear an oath of innoence. Alfonzo felt humiliated and didn't forgive El Cid for this. "El Cid and King Alfonzo: The oath at the church of Saint Agatha in Burgos" by Armando Menocal

"A battle against the Moors" by Karl Friedrich Lessing

El Cid and his knights crossed the mountains into the land of the Moors. They captured the Moorish city of Alcocer and settled down there. The Moorish king of Valencia sent three thousand horsemen to recapture the town. After a siege, El Cid and his knights came out of the gates of Alcocer, and cut their way through the army of the Moors, killing thirteen hundred enemy soldiers in a fierce battle.

Meanwhile King Alfonzo asked El Cid to return from exile. He gave him seven castles as a gift, and asked him to lead the army of Castile to reconquer Spanish lands held by the Moors, including the cities of Toledo and Valencia. El Cid gathered a large army and attacked Toledo. After a long siege the city fell, and the Moors fled. El Cid was a talented military commander. He never stopped studying the military tactics of great conquerors of the past. He ordered that books by ancient Greek and Roman authors describing famous battles be read to his troops for inspiration. El Cid also gathered his knights before every battle and worked out a plan, taking advice from anyone who came up with a good idea. Because of this teamwork, his attack tactics were different every single time, always taking his enemy by surprise.

El Cid

Valencia was one of the richest cities in Moorish Spain. El Cid knew it would be hard to capture. He sent out a call for any man from any land to join his army. He promised to share with his soldiers the treasures of the Valencia Moors:

Who wants from poverty to flee and earn a rich reward?
Let him choose a soldier's life and call El Cid his lord.
Valencia will be besieged, its walls will go down,
So Cid may to the Christians, deliver back their town.

To stop El Cid's army, the Moors flooded the plain
around Valencia by opening the floodgates
of the streams running down from nearby hills.
But El Cid cleverly led his army up into
the hills instead. They took the high ground
surrounding Valencia and blocked all the roads
leading into the city.
My lord El Cid, Rodrigo, went forth without delay.
The high walls of Valencia stood proud in his way.
He ordered it surrounded, by siege he sought to win.
Nobody could go out. Nobody could go in.

El Cid takes Valencia

A great famine broke out in Valencia. People ate horses, dogs, cats and mice, until there were only three horses and a mule left alive in the entire city. Then on June 15, 1094, the governor of Valencia arrived at El Cid's camp and handed El Cid the keys to the city. Cid commanded his men that as they take the city, they should show honor to the Moors in Valencia, greet them, and do no harm to them. El Cid made Valencia his home and called himself the Prince of Valencia. When the king of Morocco heard of this he sent an army of fifty thousand Moors to retake the city. They crossed from Africa to Spain and approached Valencia. But El Cid and his knights surprised the Moors with a clever attack and chased them to the river Guadalquivir where fifteen thousand enemy soldiers drowned.

El Cid became powerful and wealthy. He never forgot the money lenders who had lent him the six hundred marks, and made sure to repay them at his first opportunity. He was a generous ruler, respected by both Christians and Muslims in Valencia. El Cid allowed Muslims to build mosques and to worship God according to their faith. Both Christians and Muslims served in the army and in the government of Valencia under El Cid's rule. But as the years passed, El Cid grew older and became sick. He couldn't lead his soldiers into battle anymore.

In 1099 the Moors besieged Valencia again. El Cid sent his army to break the siege, but his troops were defeated and destroyed almost to the last man. A Moorish writer said that when El Cid heard the news of his army's defeat, "he died of rage." It's more likely, however, that El Cid died as a result of the famine and epidemic diseases caused by the siege. Three years later Valencia was seized by the Moors and it did not become a Christian city again for over 125 years.

The period of Spanish history between the Islamic conquest of Spain in 711 and the victory of the Christian kingdoms in 1492 is known as the **Reconquista**. It was a long series of wars and battles between the Christians and the Muslims. When King Ferdinand of Aragon and Queen Isabella I of Castile were married in 1469, Spain was united. Isabella and Ferdinand turned their joint forces on the last Muslim kingdom in Spain – the Emirate of Granada. They took it back in 1492, finishing the Reconquista. By the way, that very year Ferdinand and Isabella funded the expedition of Christopher Columbus!

"Moors surrender Granada to Ferdinand and Isabella" by Francisco Pradilla y Ortiz

Thomas Becket
1119 – 1170

In 1154, Henry II, a great-grandson of William the Conqueror, became king of England. In addition to England, Henry II ruled a big portion of France. As a result he was so busy that they said of him, "He never sits down; he is on his feet from morning till night." His chief advisor was Thomas Becket. In 1155 the king appointed Thomas Becket the Lord Chancellor of England.

At that time English clergy – bishops, priests, monks, and nuns – had become almost independent of the king. It was almost as if there were two rulers – the king and the church. King Henry wanted to bring the church under his authority. To achieve this he decided to make Thomas Becket Archbishop of Canterbury, the head of the Church in England. In 1162 Becket became a priest, and later that year he was elected Archbishop of Canterbury. The king expected that Becket would obey his commands. But now that he served the church, Becket realized that the church should be independent from the king, and should be able to correct the king if the king was wrong. In no time King Henry and Thomas Becket became enemies.

In 1164 the assembly of church leaders joined forces with the king and demanded that Thomas Becket recognize the authority of the king over the church, or there would be consequences. Becket refused to sign the documents prepared by the assembly. He was accused of contempt of royal authority and fled to France to escape the king's anger. He stayed in France for 6 years, until Henry invited him to come back to England. Soon, however, the king and Thomas Becket clashed again.

King Henry II

"The murder of Thomas Becket" by A. Dawant

One day, while surrounded by a group of knights, King Henry exclaimed in anger: "Is there no one who will rid me of this turbulent priest?" The **turbulent priest** was Thomas Becket, of course. Four knights who heard this thought the king wanted Becket to be dead. They made a plan to murder Becket. On December 29, 1170 they arrived in Canterbury, and having approached Canterbury Cathedral, they put their weapons under a mulberry tree outside, and hid their armor under their cloaks. Then they found Archbishop Thomas Becket and demanded that he obey the wishes of the king. Becket refused.

Gervase, a monk at Canterbury, who knew Thomas Becket, wrote: "After a long discussion, they began to threaten him. Finally, they went out into the courtyard, took off the cloaks that covered their armor, and, armed, headed to the Cathedral." Meanwhile the Archbishop didn't listen to priests and monks who begged him to flee. He prepared to perform the evening service. "He walked with a slow and deliberate step, like one who of his own free will prepares himself for death," says Gervase. The monks tried to bolt the door for safety, but Becket said to them, "It is not right to make a fortress out of the house of prayer!" and ordered them to reopen the doors.

The four knights with drawn swords, ran into the cathedral shouting, "Where is Thomas Becket, traitor to King and country?" Becket answered, "Here am I – no traitor, but a priest of god." Edward Grim, an eyewitness, who was with Thomas Becket at the cathedral, wrote: "'Then you,' the murderers said, 'will now die.' 'And I,' said Thomas Becket, 'am prepared to die for my Lord, so that in my blood the church will gain liberty and peace; but in the name of Almighty God I forbid that you hurt my men in any way. If it is me you seek, let them leave.'"
Then the murderers attacked Becket and killed him, breaking his skull with a sword.

When King Henry heard of the murder, he was scared. He declared that he had had nothing to do with it. Becket's murderers went into hiding for a year. Pope Alexander excommunicated them. Excommunication is a punishment prohibiting a member of the Christian church from receiving communion. Seeking forgiveness, the four knights traveled to Rome. The Pope ordered them to go to the Holy Land, and serve there for 14 years to pay for their crime. The church declared Thomas Becket a martyr – a person who sacrifices his life for his faith – and a saint.
His tomb became a holy site.

Meanwhile King Henry started having one problem after another. In 1173 his sons rebelled against him. And his wife, Eleanor of Aquitaine, supported them against her husband. France, Brittany, Scotland and other countries sent their troops to support the rebellion. Henry thought that God was punishing him for the murder of Thomas Becket. He decided to ask God and Thomas Becket for forgiveness and went to visit the Archbishop's tomb in Canterbury Cathedral. On the road to Canterbury Cathedral where Becket was buried the king took off his hat and his shoes and walked barefoot. The next day he put whips into the hands of the cathedral monks and said, "Whip me as I kneel at the tomb of the saint." The monks did as he requested.

"The penance of KIng Henry II at the tomb of Thomas Becket" by Samuel Seeberger

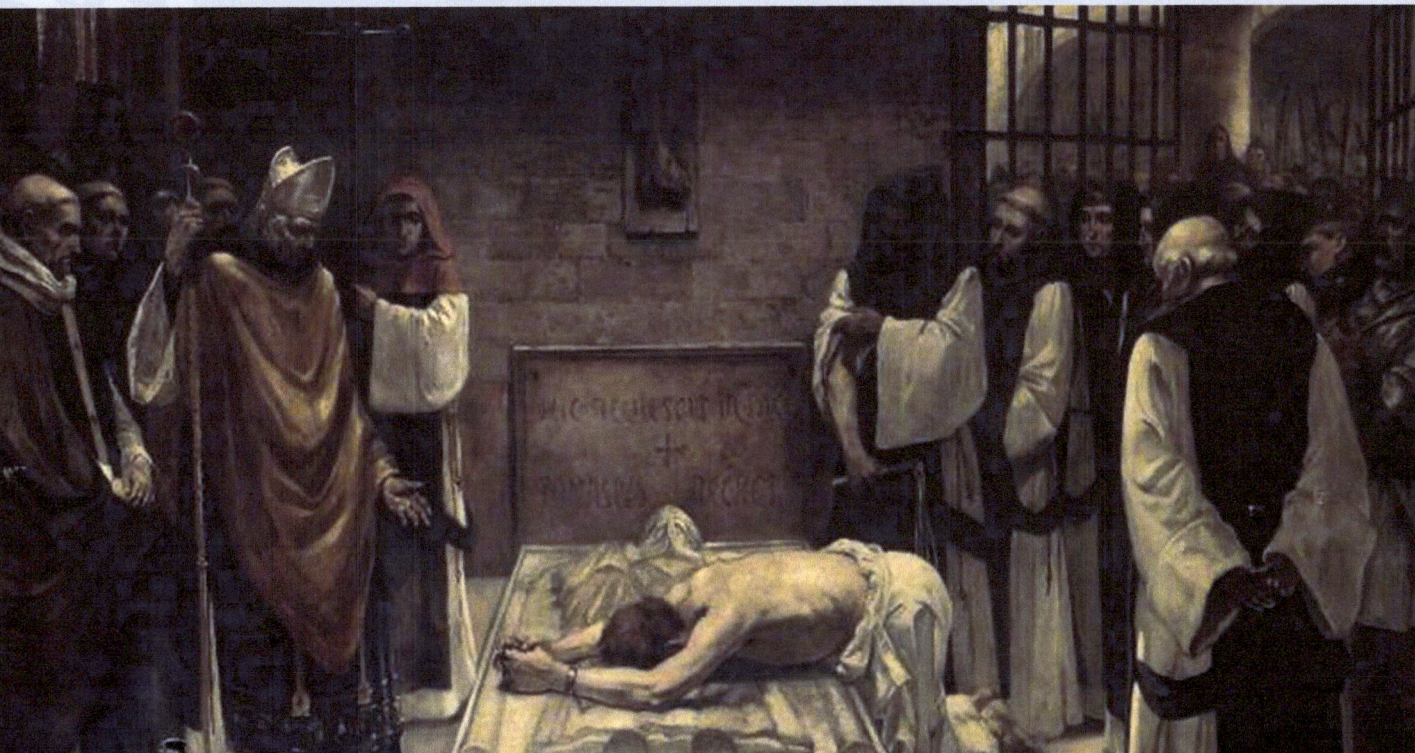

Reliquary box showing the scene of the murder of Thomas Becket. Reliquaries are boxes that hold relics. Relics are objects that have a direct connection to a holy person, such as a Christian saint. A relic can be the saint's hair, or some of their remains, such as bones, or personal things that belonged to a saint. Reliquaries were very popular in the Middle Ages.

Soon after, King Henry defeated his sons and locked up his wife as a prisoner. Peace followed for some years, but in the last year of his life the King's troubles returned. His oldest son, Henry, rebelled against him again, and soon died.

King Henry's favorite son was John, but his wife Eleanor's favorite son was Richard (later known as **Richard the Lionheart**). Concerned that the old king would give his throne to John, Richard took up arms against the king in 1188. He was supported by the king of France. King Henry was defeated. The king was very ill, and when he saw the list of Englishmen who had joined Richard in his rebellion, he found among them the name of his favorite son John. His heart was broken, and he died a few days later.

In the Middle Ages cathedrals became places where people could go to study the arts, history, law, and medicine. Many cathedrals opened schools that later became universities. Europe's oldest universities were the University of Bologna in Italy, the University of Paris in France, and the Universities of Oxford and Cambridge in England.
All of these grew from cathedrals.

Canterbury Cathedral and an inscribed sword from the times of Richard the Lionheart. The knights of that era often had the blades of their swords inscribed with a motto or a prayer in Latin.

The word *university* comes from the Latin word *universitas* which means 'a group of people who are united into a community or a society.' As universities started growing, higher education became much more widely available in Europe.

The most famous style of medieval architecture is known as the *Gothic style*. It appeared in the early 12th century in France, and then spread to England and Germany. Among the most famous Gothic buildings still standing today are Westminster Abbey and Canterbury Cathedral in England. European architects of the Middle Ages created buildings with pointed arched ceilings supported by columns and special structures outside the building walls called *buttresses*. The weight of the ceiling was no longer resting entirely on the walls. This made possible such features of Gothic architecture as huge stained-glass windows, tall towers and spires, and lots of sculptures decorating the walls. To prevent rainwater from running down the walls, they made water spouts in the shape of monsters and dragons – called *gargoyles*. Rainwater ran out of their mouths onto the street. The name *gargoyle* comes from the Latin word *gargula* which means *throat*.

Cathedral in Cologne, Germany, and Amiens Cathedral in France

A gargoyle

ELEANOR OF AQUITAINE

1122 – 1204

Eleanor's father was the Duke of Aquitaine. Aquitaine was the largest and richest province of France. Eleanor grew up at her parents' glamorous court of Poitiers. She was given an excellent education: She learned math, history, and astronomy, which was unusual for women in those days. She also took lessons in the art of conversation, dance, chess, playing the harp, and singing. Eleanor was intelligent and beautiful. French *troubadour* (poet and singer) Bernard de Ventadour called her "gracious, lovely, charm itself," with "lovely eyes and a noble appearance."

"Queen Eleanor" by Anthony Frederick Sandys

In 1137 Eleanor's father died. Only 15 years old, Eleanor became the Duchess of Aquitaine. On his deathbed, Eleanor's father asked Louis, the king of France, to be the guardian of his daughter. But Louis had his own plan: He ordered Eleanor to marry his 17-year-old son – whose name was also Louis – to bring Aquitaine under the control of the French crown. So Eleanor and Prince Louis were married. Only a few days after the wedding King Louis died. On Christmas day that year Prince Louis and Eleanor were crowned the King and Queen of France. Eleanor's husband was in love with her and fulfilled her every wish, but many around him thought Eleanor was too much into fashion and adventures, and was a bad influence.

Louis was quiet and religious. He was not really interested in being a ruler. Eleanor, on the other hand, was ready to be the queen. She attended her husband's council meetings and often argued with his advisors. Eleanor was bored. In those days Paris was a small town with a population of only about 10,000 people. Most cities in Europe were far from glamorous at that time. Eleanor brought with her to Paris the fashions and customs of Aquitaine, and started redecorating the royal palace. She ordered amazing dresses to be designed for her for every court event and holiday. Louis wore simple old clothes. He shaved off his curly hair. Eleanor complained that he looked more like a monk than a king. She complained that he was gloomy and boring. Soon the marriage of Louis and Eleanor started to look like a disaster.

Medieval French ring – gold and black enamel, 13th century

That's when they heard the call of Pope Eugenius III for the Second Crusade. **Crusades** were military expeditions of European Christian knights to recapture the Holy Land. The **Holy Land**, or the land of ancient Israel, where Jesus Christ lived and died, had been seized by the Muslims, and Christians believed it was their duty to return the Holy Land to the authority of the Catholic church.

The word *crusade* comes from the French *croisade* – the way of the cross. There were many crusades. The symbol of the Crusaders was a red cross. Soldiers wore it on their shields and armor. Their battle cry was "Deus vult!" – Latin, meaning "God wills it."

In the First Crusade, European knights successfully conquered Jerusalem, the capital of ancient Israel. That was in 1099. By 1144 the Muslims had captured most of the Holy Land again. That's when Pope Eugenius III issued his call for the Second Crusade – to push the Muslim forces back once again.

Meanwhile the young King Louis was getting into trouble with the church. His soldiers had stormed a town and set on fire a cathedral where fifteen hundred people had taken refuge. Many people perished in the flames. Churches were used as **sanctuaries** – authorities were not allowed to injure or kill a person inside a church. To wipe away his guilt Louis decided to take part in the Second Crusade. Eleanor, who was 19, thought of it as an adventure and announced she would go with him to the Holy Land.

"King Louis and Queen Eleanor receive the banner of the crusade" by Jean-Baptiste Mauzaisse

"Crusaders approach Antioch" by Frederic-Henri Schopin

Eleanor was to be accompanied by 1000 knights, 300 ladies, and a large group of minstrels and troubadours. The ladies were dressed in special costumes that looked like armor, with spears that were not real, but looked cool and shiny. Eleanor was a fan of Greek mythology and wanted her court ladies to look like Amazons, legendary female warriors. Most crusaders in Louis' army thought Eleanor was acting in bad taste. Crusades were similar to a pilgrimage – a journey to a holy site – only on a crusade, each knight was prepared to give his life for his faith. There was hardly enough food and water for the crusaders during their long and exhausting journey. They were not amused by ladies in costumes and an endless caravan of their baggage filled with dresses and fancy household stuff. They were so upset about Eleanor that after the Second Crusade the pope released a papal *edict*, an order in which he forbade women to ever join crusades.

The Crusaders made their way to Constantinople, the capital of Byzantium. From there they headed to Jerusalem. On their way Louis sent Eleanor and her ladies with half of his army to make a camp on top of a hill, while he took the rest of his knights to push back the Muslim forces that had been attacking them along the way. But Eleanor didn't like the hill. She ordered the camp to be made in a lovely green valley below. This allowed the enemy to take the hill, separate the two halves of the French army and, after a long battle, nearly destroy them. Those who survived escaped to Antalia, where Louis tried to hire ships to carry them to the Holy Land. But there were not enough ships. Louis abandoned his army, and with his friends sailed to Antioch in Syria.
Most of his soldiers, left behind, were either killed or captured by the Muslims.
Finally the crusaders returned to France, where Louis and Eleanor divorced in 1152.
A few weeks later Eleanor married Prince Henry of Anjou.

Eleanor was 30, Henry was 18. Two years later Eleanor's new husband became King Henry II of England and Eleanor became the queen of England! In England Eleanor was even more of a fashion influencer. During the crusade she had bought a lot of dresses, veils, belts, and other accessories in Constantinople and Antioch. She brought these eastern fashions with her to England. Her English court ladies started copying her style.

Henry and Eleanor had 8 kids – 5 sons and 3 daughters. Two of their sons became kings, first Richard the Lionheart, who was Eleanor's favorite son, and then John, who was Henry's favorite son, and may be familiar to you as the evil King Henry from the legend of Robin Hood.

Henry and Eleanor ruled their kingdom as a team. Henry ruled England and Eleanor ruled their lands in France. In 1168 Eleanor moved to Poitiers in France, and stayed there for five years. Eleanor's court in Poitiers is probably the most famous royal court of the Middle Ages.
It was there where many medieval court customs and fashions emerged.
Eleanor welcomed traveling poets and singers – minstrels and troubadours – who sung tales of King Arthur and the Knights of the Round Table. Chretien de Troyes, the author of **Perceval, the Story of the Grail**, was one of Eleanor's court poets.

*Above: "The Dedication" by Edmund Blair Leighton.
A knight leaving on a crusade dedicates his sword to a saint.*

*Right: "God Speed" by Edmund Blair Leighton.
A knight is leaving on a crusade. A lady ties a scarf on his arm - a symbol of love and loyalty.*

Eleanor's court was one of the places where the ideas of *chivalry* were formed, later to spread across Europe. Thanks to Christian teachings about compassion and selfless love, people in Medieval Europe started to see kindness, charity, and loyalty as more important than courage, cleverness, power, or riches. Chivalry was a set of rules for knights and their families that appeared between 1170 and 1220. Among the rules of chivalry were these:

- Respect those who are weaker than you and defend them.
- Never lie, and always keep your word.
- Be generous (give more than you take), and be charitable (sacrifice to help others).
- Always protect Good against Evil, Right against Wrong.

The rules of chivalry also said that a knight must treat any woman with great respect, not in the same way he would treat a man, but with greater respect and politeness.

"The Shadow" by Edmund Blair Leighton.
A lady traces the shadow of a knight leaving on a crusade.

Chivalry changed people's idea of love. Love was now viewed as a source of inspiration that motivated knights to heroic deeds that would bring a person closer to God. Stories of knights' *tournaments* (fighting competitions) tell us that they would put their life in danger to look like a hero in the eyes of a lady they were in love with.

After the murder of Thomas Becket, Eleanor and her oldest son revolted against King Henry, but their plot failed. Eleanor tried to escape to Paris dressed as a knight, but Henry's men captured her and imprisoned her in Touraine. Over the next 15 years she remained a prisoner until King Henry died and Richard freed her from captivity. In 1189, when Eleanor was 67 years old, she arrived at Westminster Abbey to watch her son Richard the Lionheart be crowned the English king.

However, Richard was less interested in ruling his lands than in fighting on crusade. He sailed off to the Holy Land, leaving Eleanor in charge of his kingdom. While Richard was away, Eleanor's son John tried to seize his brother's throne, and French King Phillip II attacked their kingdom in France. Eleanor fought off these threats. Then another disaster happened. Richard the Lionheart was captured and held for ransom by the Duke of Austria. Eleanor seized the gold of the church, and raised taxes to get 100,000 marks for Richard's release. Richard was freed, but in 1199 he was wounded in battle and died in his mother's arms. Eleanor named her son John king, but she didn't trust him, so she kept control over the French portion of the kingdom to keep him in check.

Eleanor lived to the age of 82. She never stopped traveling and negotiating support for King John.

Left: Richard the Lionheart and King John

Right: A crystal and gold vase given by Eleanor to Louis VII.

Below: Castle of the Dukes of Aquitaine in Poitier. Queen Eleanor held her court in the great hall called The Hall of the Lost Footsteps.

RICHARD THE LIONHEART
1157 – 1199

Richard the Lionheart became the king of England in 1189. Raised by his French mother, Eleanor of Aquitaine, he spoke only French! Richard was very well-educated. He wrote music and poetry. Even before he was crowned king, Richard was respected as a talented leader and a warrior of rare courage. His bravery earned him the nickname that made him a legend – the *Lionheart*, or *Cœur de Lion* in French. As soon as he became king he started planning a war against Saladin, the leader of the Muslim forces, or *the Saracens* as they were often called in those days. Saladin had recaptured Jerusalem in 1187, and Richard couldn't wait for the Third Crusade.

*"Richard Leaving England for the Crusades, 1189"
by Glyn Warren Philpot*

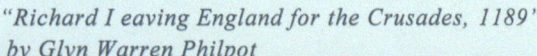

He raised money for war by draining the royal treasury, raising taxes, and by selling government positions and offices. "I would sell the city of London if I could find a purchaser," he said.

In October of 1187 Sultan Saladin entered Jerusalem, tore down the cross that had been erected on the Temple Mount, and sent it as a present to the Caliph of Baghdad. The Caliph dug it into the ground outside the city gates, so that it was level with the road. Everyone who traveled by that road had to step on the cross. When this news reached Rome, Pope Gregory VIII proclaimed the Third Crusade. Once the crusade was announced, Richard led the joint forces of the European kingdoms to the Holy Land. The French and English Crusaders together numbered more than one hundred thousand men. Between the second and the third Crusades, military religious orders such as the **Teutonic Knights** and the **Knights Templar** were formed. Their job was to protect pilgrims on their way to the Holy Land, to build hospitals, and to support crusades. They joined the Third Crusade as well.

Every night at the crusaders' camp the heralds blew their trumpets, and called out three times, "Save the Holy Sepulchre!" Every night the crusaders knelt and said, "Amen!" *Sepulcher* means *tomb*. *The Holy Sepulcher* was the site of the resurrection of Jesus Christ, his empty tomb, with a church built over it.

"The surrender of Acre to Richard the Lionheart and Philippe Auguste of France" – by Merry-Joseph Blondel

Richard was so fearless that once, before a battle, he rode up to the enemy line and called for anyone to step forth and fight him one-on-one. None among the Saracens responded to the challenge. Once Saladin's brother saw Richard in a battle, fighting in the front lines. Richard's horse was killed. Saladin's brother was so impressed with Richard's courage that he sent him two of his best horses as a gift.

Richard's army took the town of Acre thanks to a mysterious friend inside the city. An arrow frequently came down from the walls of Acre with a letter wound around the arrow shaft. The letter was always addressed to Richard. The writer said he was a Christian and in his letters he shared information about the plans of the Saracens besieged in Acre. Richard won back some other lands that had been lost to Saladin but he failed to take back Jerusalem. Instead he signed a peace treaty with Saladin by which the Christians had the right to visit Jerusalem for 3 years without paying any fees to Saladin.

"Sultan Saladin" by Cristofano Dell Altissimo

In 1192 Richard headed back home. His journey home was difficult. His ship was caught in a storm in the Adriatic Sea and shipwrecked near Venice. To get to England he had to cross the lands of Leopold, duke of Austria, one of his enemies.

"Richard the Lionheart at the Battle of Arsuf" by Éloi Firmin Féron

During the crusade, at Acre, the Duke had set his banner upon a tower that he had taken, and Richard, who couldn't stand the Duke, had torn it down and flung it into a ditch. To avoid Leopold's soldiers, King Richard dressed as a poor pilgrim returning from the Holy Land. But not far from Vienna he was recognized because his servant didn't count money when buying food at the market, and people noticed that Richard wore a precious ring only a king could afford. Richard was captured by Leopold and locked up in a castle. Leopold kept secret the place where Richard was imprisoned.

A legend says that Richard was found by one of his knights, named Blondel, who pretended to be a minstrel and went from castle to castle in Austria singing Richard's favorite songs. One day a girl came up to him saying she knew the song he was singing: A prisoner in the North Tower of the castle up the road sang it often, she said. At night Blondel approached the castle and sang the song by the North Tower. He heard the song refrain repeated from a window of a castle and recognized King Richard's voice.

While in prison, Richard wrote a ballad *Ja nus hons pris – No prisoner*. A **ballad** is a song that tells a story. Written in French, Richard's ballad opens with these words:

No prisoner can tell his honest thought
Unless he speaks as one who suffers wrong.
But in his sorrow he's free to make a song.
So many friends... but I've been waiting long
For help. Shame on them if they leave me here
For yet another year.

Richard's portrait on his tomb in Anjou, France

Once the place of Richard's imprisonment became known, many European kings and warlords demanded his release. Imprisoning a crusader was against the law in most lands. Pope Celestine III excommunicated Duke Leopold. Then Leopold handed Richard over to the German King Henry VI – who also refused to let him go. Pope Celestine excommunicated Henry VI. Richard had little respect for the German king. When asked to recognize Henry's authority, Richard responded, "I am born of a rank which recognises no superior but God."

Ruins of the Dürnstein Castle in Austria where Richard the Lionheart was held captive

Finally, Henry VI agreed to let Richard go if his family paid him 150,000 silver marks. The medieval Chronicle of the Third Crusade *Itinerary of Richard I and others to the Holy Land* says that "To gather the money for his ransom, the taxes in England were raised above all limits. Cups and sacred vessels of gold and silver were gathered from the churches, and the monasteries had to give up their gold." The ransom was paid, and Richard returned to England in 1194.

In Richard's absence his brother John revolted with the help of the French king Philip, who conquered Normandy. When Richard was released, the French king sent a message to John, "The devil is free again." Upon his return, Richard forgave his brother, but started a war against Philip. He won one victory after another. Philip fled. Richard made the French words *Dieu et mon Droit* – God and my Right – his motto. In the Middle Ages most noble families had their own emblem, called *the coat of arms*, and a motto – words that tell the idea most important to the family. Richard's motto – still part of the British royal coat of arms today – echoed the words he said to Henry VI – that he had no superior but God. Richard also adopted the image of 3 lions as the royal emblem of England. Family, city, and state emblems like this are called *heraldic* designs.

One of the Robin Hood legends, *Robin Hood and Richard the Lionheart* says that King Richard wanted to meet Robin Hood and went to the famous Sherwood forest looking for him. But Robin Hood was nowhere to be found. Why? "If you were a monk or an abbot traveling through Sherwood forest, you would meet him right away," said one of the king's friends, " He often robs monks and abbots because the monasteries rob the poor by making them pay heavy taxes."

Hearing this, King Richard dressed like an abbot, and with his knights dressed like monks, he went back to Sherwood forest.

*"Robin Hood" by N.C.Wyeth
and the British Royal coat of arms*

Robin Hood and his men attacked them, but Richard said he was the king's messenger. He showed Robin the ring he used to give to messengers as proof that they were sent by the king himself. Robin Hood invited Richard to a dinner in the forest. The king liked Robin Hood, revealed himself, and offered him a royal pardon. Robin Hood and his men left the forest and joined the king's army. But after Richard the LIonheart died, his brother, the evil King John once again declared Robin an outlaw. Robin Hood and his men went back to Sherwood forest.

On March 26, 1199, Richard was wounded by an arrow shot from a crossbow, and died. The person who shot him turned out to be a boy. Richard had killed the boy's father and two brothers, and the boy wanted revenge. On his deathbed Richard asked to see the boy and forgave him, saying "Live on, and through my generosity see the light of day." He ordered that the boy be given 100 shillings and let go.

Following Richard's death, his brother John became king in 1199. After his barons revolted against him, King John made an agreement with them that became known as the **Magna Carta** – the **Great Charter**, in Latin. The Magna Carta named all the rights that belonged to the citizens of England and King John promised that none of these rights would ever be taken away. Among other things, it stated: "No man shall be arrested or imprisoned, except by the judgement of their equals and by the law of the land."

The Castle of Montbrun where Richard the Lionheart died in 1199.
Richard the Lionheart's heraldic emblem.

The rebels appointed a council of 25 barons to see that the king fulfilled the promises of the Magna Carta. That council eventually became the Parliament of England. The ideas of the Magna Carta influenced the political development of other countries. The American colonists used the rights the Magna Carta guaranteed as one of their reasons to rebel and form their own country. Many of these rights were included in the United States Constitution and Bill of Rights.

The social system of the Middle Ages is known as *feudalism* or the *feudal system*. The word *feudalism* comes from the medieval Latin word *feudum* which means *a fee*. At the bottom of the feudal system were people who worked on the land – farmers and *serfs*. Serfs were similar to slaves: They were not allowed to leave the land of their masters. All the land in the kingdom belonged to the king. The king would give some of the land to the lords who fought for him. The lords gave some of their land to their *vassals* – such as *earls* and *barons* – in exchange for military service and taxes. When a land owner died, all the land went to his oldest son. His younger sons became knights who served the king and lords as warriors or bodyguards. Knighthood was also often given as the reward for courage and loyalty.

The day before being *knighted*, the future knight had to take a bath, a symbol that his past wrongdoings were washed away. Then they dressed him in a white robe, the symbol of a pure heart. Over it he wore a red tunic, the symbol of his blood which he may shed fighting for his lord. On top of it he wore a black cloak – a reminder that death would come to him, as to all men. He spent the night in a church, praying alone by the altar. This was called the *vigil of arms*. He was not allowed to sit – only stand or kneel. The next day after the church service, the ceremony of *knighting* took place. It was called the *accolade*. For this, the future knight was dressed in full armor. A king or a queen touched the kneeling man's shoulder with the flat of a sword and said, "Arise, Sir Knight."

"A knight's vigil" by John Pettie

Two paintings by Edmond Blair Leighton: "Vanquished" (a knight who lost a tournament), and "The times of peril" (a knight and his family escape from being captured by their enemies)

FREDERICK BARBAROSSA
1122 – 1190

Frederick I was the most famous German king of the Middle Ages. His beard earned him his Italian nickname, *Barbarossa – red-bearded*. He came to the throne in 1152 and ruled for 35 years. Charlemagne was his inspiration. At that time Germany was made of many separate states ruled by local princes and warlords. These German states were often at war with one another. Barbarossa's lifelong goal was to make Germany a unified nation.

Some German kings before Barbarossa had called themselves emperors but nobody had ever crowned them. Frederick wanted to be crowned Emperor of the Holy Roman Empire by the Pope in Rome, like Charlemagne. In 1155 when the Pope needed some military help, Frederick offered it in exchange for his coronation. He marched into Italy burning Italian cities that resisted German rule. As his army approached Rome, Pope Adrian left the city to meet Frederick. But their meeting did not go well. According to custom, when a king met a Pope, the king had to kneel and hold the stirrup of the Pope's horse while the Pope dismounted. Also the king had to kiss the Pope's feet, and then he would receive from the Pope the kiss of peace.

A golden reliquary made as a portrait of Barbarossa, 1171

Frederick Barbarossa wanted to teach the pope who held the real power in Italy, so he refused to hold the Pope' stirrup. Then Pope Adrian refused to give Barbarossa the kiss of peace – and left. After a day of negotiations Barbarossa finally gave up. "I am doing this for Saint Peter, not for Adrian," he muttered angrily, while holding the Pope's stirrup.

The next day Barbarossa was crowned Holy Roman Emperor at Saint Peter's Basilica in Rome. Not everyone celebrated his coronation.

Some Romans started a revolt just as Frederick was being crowned at Saint Peter's. They didn't accept the authority of Barbarossa, who, they said, bought the emperor's crown from the pope. Without hesitation Frederick and his army slaughtered 1,000 Romans on that day. It is said that Barbarossa pulled out his sword and shouted to the crowd of Roman rebels:
"Here is the gold with which the German Emperor buys his crown!"

On his way back to Germany Barbarossa stopped at the castle of a knight who was secretly in the service of his enemies. The enemies made a plan to murder Barbarossa while he slept. However, the knight was so impressed with the Emperor's ideas and generosity that he felt sorry for his betrayal and admitted it to Frederick. It was too late, however. The castle had already been surrounded by the enemy troops. Then one of Barbarossa's knights, Hartmann von Siebeneichen, offered to sacrifice his own life for the king. Hartmann and Barbarossa exchanged clothes, and Barbarossa left the castle with a group of servants. At midnight the enemy entered the castle and found Hartmann sleeping in Barbarossa's bed. When they heard Hartmann's story, they admired his courage and let him go free.

Barbarossa returned to Germany, but a few years later Pope Adrian died and two rival popes were elected in Rome – Pope Alexander III and the 'antipope' Victor IV. Both sought Barbarossa's support.

"Barbarossa falls off his horse and loses the Battle of Legnano to the Lombards" by Amos Cassioli

Frederick demanded that Pope Alexander appear before him and accept his royal authority. Alexander refused. Then Barbarossa declared his support for the 'antipope' Victor. This caused more conflicts and wars in Italy, and resulted in Barbarossa's defeat by the rebels of Milan in the Italian province of Lombardy. Eventually, he had to kneel at the feet of Pope Alexander and receive the kiss of peace in order to have the support of the church.

Meanwhile, Germany was torn by continuous civil wars. It was hard to keep German warlords at peace with one another. Two warlords (one of whom was an archbishop!) had been quarreling for a long time. Their wars had devastated a few provinces. To punish both of them, Frederick sentenced them to walk a mile together, each carrying a dog on his back! Their supporters had to follow them, each carrying a chair... And peasants who worked on their lands had to follow them, each carrying a wheel. Another problem were the lawless **robber barons**, the warlords who plundered nearby villages and escaped from punishment in their mountain castles along the river Rhine. Some of them captured travelers and held them for ransom. Barbarossa fought these warlords by levelling their castles to the ground! Bit by bit, life in Germany became much safer.

"Barbarossa stops a quarrel between two warlords" by Hermann Plüdemann

When the pope announced the Third Crusade, Frederick Barbarossa decided to join it. He raised an army of 150 thousand crusaders and set out for Palestine. Barbarossa's army was so large that it could not be taken to the Middle East by sea. He took the land route. When he marched into Asia Minor he attacked the forces of Saladin, and defeated them in two great battles.

"Barbarossa at the battle of Iconium, Third Crusade," by Hermann Wislicenus

But these were Barbarossa's last victories. When his army was crossing a bridge over a river, and the bridge was crowded, Frederick rode his horse into the river, expecting that it would swim across. But his horse was knocked off its feet by the strong current of the river. Wearing heavy armor, Barbarossa was unable to swim, and he drowned. Here is how the author of the **Itinerary of Richard I and others to the Holy Land** described the death of Frederick: "While the horses and baggage were passing this river, the victorious emperor stopped. He was indeed an illustrious man, moderately tall, with red hair and beard; his head was partly turning grey, his eyes sparkling; his chest and shoulders were broad. This great man became impatient about the delay and directed his horse into the stream. O sea! O earth! O heaven! The Emperor in whom the glory of ancient Rome again flourished, was overwhelmed by the waters and perished!"

There are many legends of Frederick Barbarossa. One of them is the legend of him as a **sleeping hero**. Many people believed that Frederick was not really dead, but only asleep in a cave in the German mountains. Inside the cave under the mountain, he was said to be sitting on his throne at a table. His red beard had grown through the table! His knights were standing around him, also asleep.

From time to time Barbarossa lifted his hand and sent a servant boy to see if the ravens had stopped flying around the mountain. "When the ravens stop flying around the mountain," said the legend, "Barbarossa shall awake and restore Germany to its ancient greatness."

"Barbarossa awakens" by Hermann Wislicenus

St. Francis of Assisi
1182 – 1226

"St. Francis" by Francesco Francia

Saint Francis, or Francis of Assisi, was a Catholic *friar* who established the Franciscan Order of friars. Friars were monks who didn't live in a monastery, but traveled around, preaching the Christian faith and doing other work for the church. St. Francis' birth name was Giovanni di Pietro di Bernardone. His father was a silk merchant in the Italian town of Assisi. Even though the baby's name was Giovanni, his father called him Francesco – **the Frenchman** – or Francis – because his wife was French and he loved France and French culture. The family was wealthy, and as Francis grew up, he got used to spending money on expensive clothes and rare wines. He was well-educated, wrote poetry, and had many friends. He learned by heart many songs that he heard performed by troubadours, the wandering poets and singers. His favorites were ballads about King Arthur, the Knights of the Round Table, and Charlemagne.

One day, as Francis was working in his father's shop, a ragged, hungry beggar knocked on the door. Francis was spreading out beautiful silks and velvets before his father's customers. The beggar asked for food. "Please, in the name of God," he muttered. Francis told him to leave, but moments later he felt ashamed that he had so little compassion. He rushed out of the shop, found the beggar and gave him all the money he had in his pockets. On his way home he started noticing things he had never noticed before. The streets were full of people who looked hungry, overworked, or sick. "These people could live for months on the money that I waste in just one day," thought Francis. His rich friends laughed at him when they heard the story of the beggar, and his father scolded him in rage.

Francis started feeling ashamed of his carefree life. Around 1202, inspired by the stories of Charlemagne, he joined the army, went on a military expedition, and was taken prisoner. He spent a year in captivity. These experiences changed Francis. He was no longer sure he wanted to be a great warrior.

Carved elephant tusk used as a drinking vessel, Italy, 12th century. The design includes an image of a lamb, a symbol of Christ.

"Francis goes to war" and, below: *"Francis gives his clothes to a beggar"* by Pedro Subercaseaux

But he didn't know what other path he could follow, so he went back to his carefree life in Assisi and soon joined another military campaign. One night, while traveling with his fellow soldiers, Francis had a strange vision. Among other things, he saw scenes of war, with men dying, women crying, kids begging for bread, and cities lying in ruins. He was overwhelmed with compassion for the poor, the suffering, the sick, and the prisoners...

He wanted to feed, clothe, heal and comfort them all. Francis gave up his military career and decided to make a trip to Rome, the seat of the Pope and the Catholic Church.

In Rome, Francis went to visit the Church of St. Peter. On the steps of the church a crowd of dirty beggars pulled at the clothes of people entering the church, weeping and asking for money. "Here, in Rome, where there are so many men who are rich, wise, and holy, is there no one to help the poor?" wondered Francis. Suddenly he knew the path he must follow. He gave one of the beggars money and, with no explanation, asked to exchange clothes with him. The beggar traded his rags for the fancy clothes of a wealthy youth, and Francis returned to the steps of St.Peter's dressed as a beggar. He sat by the door of the church and begged. When he returned home, his family and friends thought he had gone mad. His father was angry.

A 12th-century prayer book manuscript that belonged to St. Francis of Assisi

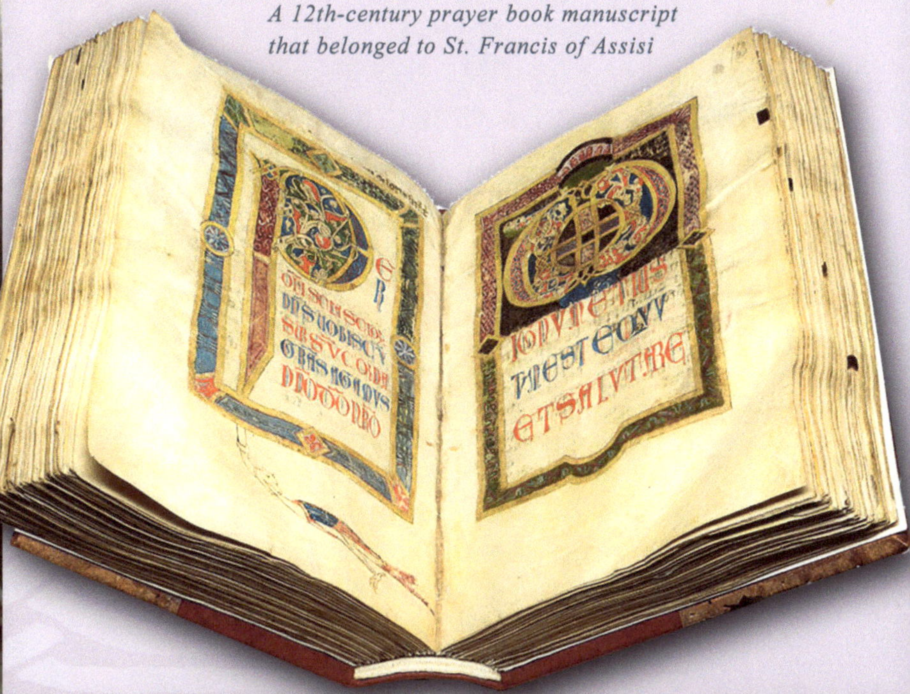

One day, when Francis wandered into the abandoned Chapel of San Damiano in the countryside near Assisi, it seemed to him that Jesus Christ looked at him from a painting on the wall. He heard the voice of Jesus saying, "Francis, go and repair my house which, as you can see, is falling into ruins." Francis thought that Jesus was talking about the abandoned chapel. He ran home, took some silk cloth from his father's shop, quickly sold it, and brought a few gold coins to the priest at San Damiano. When the priest learned that Francis had taken the silk without his father's permission, he refused to accept the gift. Upset, Francis threw the gold on the ground and left. He was afraid to go home, so he spent a whole month hiding in caves near Assisi. Finally, cold and hungry, he came back and knocked on the door of his house. His father grabbed Francis, bound him with a rope and locked him up in a store room. Only when Francis' father had left on a business trip did Francis' mom let him out.

Francis became homeless, wandering around dressed in old clothes given to him by the gardener of a local bishop. Every day he begged for stones to rebuild San Damiano's chapel. Whenever he got a stone, he carried it to the old chapel and set it in place. Bit by bit the chapel walls grew. In the course of 2 years he restored a few ruined chapels around Assisi. He said that he served Lady Poverty. Many still thought that he was insane. Children often threw mud and stones at him. His former friends laughed at him. But at the hospital where he helped to take care of the sick, they called him Brother Francis and appreciated his deep compassion and endless patience.

Soon Francis became famous for his holy life, and people he had never met before started coming to him and asking him to teach them how to live their life in poverty and prayer, like him. Even some of his rich friends from Assisi had a change of heart. Bernardo di Quintevalle, a childhood friend of Francis', gave away his money and property and came to live with Francis. Francis called him Brother Bernardo. Within a year there were 11 brothers, or *friars*. They lived under the open skies, worked at hospitals for free, preached Christian teachings, and begged for food. A rich abbot who lived near Assisi heard about the brothers and gave them a plot of land with an old chapel. There they built a few huts, planted a hedge, and it became their home. Francis wore a simple woolen tunic, like the ones worn by the poorest Italian peasants. He used a knotted rope as a belt. Other friars started dressing like him. Francis had only one rule for his friars:
"Follow the teachings of our Lord Jesus Christ and walk in his footsteps".

The city of Assisi.

"St. Francis preaching to the birds" by Giotto

Francis spent a lot of time in the woods and fields. He said that nature was the mirror of God. When the friars planted a vegetable garden, Francis asked them to leave a corner of the garden for "our little sisters, the wild flowers." There are many stories about St. Francis' love for animals. He bought two doves at the market and set them free. He saved a bunny from a trap. He threw a fish given to him for dinner back into the river. One day when Francis was preaching to a crowd in the street, so many swallows were flying overhead and their shrill calls were so loud that Francis addressed them saying, "It is my turn to talk, little sisters! Be quiet and listen until I have finished." The legend says the swallows obeyed and immediately fell silent.

Here is a story of St. Francis and a wolf. In the village of Gubbio, a wolf had been stealing sheep and killing the shepherds' dogs. Nobody dared to go outside at night. Francis told the villagers he would go talk to the wolf and walked straight into the woods. A few terrified villagers followed at a distance behind him. Soon they saw the wolf. As it headed toward Francis, Francis said: "Brother wolf, I ask you, for Christ's sake, do no harm to me, nor to any one." To the villagers' surprise the wolf stopped and lay on the ground! "You have committed many crimes, hurting and killing God's creatures," continued Francis, talking to the wolf. "Not only have you killed and eaten beasts, but you have dared to attack men, made in God's image, and, therefore, you deserve to be punished like the worst of murderers. But I wish to make peace between you and the folk of this village." Francis invited the wolf to come to the village square and the wolf followed him there! On the square, Francis asked the wolf to put his paw on his hand as a sign of peace. The wolf obeyed. The story goes on to say that from that very day the wolf stopped stealing sheep. Instead, the wolf would come to the village, and be fed by the villagers.

At that time Francis was neither a monk nor a priest, and did not have official permission to preach or perform church rites. So in 1209 he led his 11 followers to Rome, hoping to receive permission from Pope Innocent III to form a new **religious order**. A **religious order** is a community of people following a particular religious practice. Many religious orders are groups of monks. The Pope agreed to give the new **Franciscan Order** his blessing. He also gave his blessing to another new order – the **Dominican Order**, founded by St. Dominic.

"St. Francis" by Giovanni Bellini

Francis and his followers were **tonsured**. **Tonsure** was a practice of shaving hair off the top of one's head as a symbol of humility. Franciscan brothers did not own any property, and did not decorate their churches. While amazing Gothic cathedrals rose all over Europe, Franciscan churches were small and made from the cheapest materials. Many men who joined the Franciscans begged Francis to allow them to spend their wealth on churches. But Francis was firm.
"The money you give our order is for the poor, and to the poor it must go.'
Only 10 years later the Franciscan Order had 5000 members.

When the Fifth Crusade was announced, Francis went along with the crusaders to Egypt. He wanted to meet the Muslim ruler of Egypt, Sultan al-Kamil, and preach to him the teaching of Christ. Sultan al-Kamil was a nephew of Saladin.

After one of the battles, Francis and one of his friars secretly crossed into enemy territory. They were instantly captured by the Sultan's guards and brought before the Sultan. It's not known how the meeting between Francis and Sultan al-Kamil went. However, St. Bonaventure who wrote *Life of St. Francis of Assisi* about 40 years after these events, tells us that while at the Muslims' camp, Francis got into an argument with the Sultan's *astrologers*. An *astrologer* is a fortune-teller who predicts the future by interpreting the positions of planets and stars. The Sultan's astrologers laughed at Francis, so he asked the Sultan: "My lord, tell your slaves to build here a fire. It may be that God will show us a sign." When the fire blazed high, Francis spoke to the astrologers: "If you love your religion more than your life, walk into the midst of this fire with me." The Sultan was amazed at the courage of Francis. The astrologers were frightened and begged the Sultan to send Francis away. The Fifth Crusade was not successful. It was not until the Sixth Crusade in 1229 that al-Kamil surrendered Jerusalem to Christian rule.

Back in Italy, the Franciscan order was growing. One day, in 1224, while deep in prayer, Francis saw a vision of a six-winged angel. When it was over, he discovered wounds on his hands, feet, and in his side. Nobody could explain how these wounds appeared on his body. Such wounds, similar to the crucifixion wounds of Jesus, are called *stigmata*. The Catholic Church views them as a sign of holiness. Francis was the first in the history of the church to experience stigmata.

Francis died in 1226, singing *Psalm 141* – a beautiful prayer song from the *Old Testament* of the *Bible*.

The house in Assisi where St. Francis grew up

I call to you, Lord, come quickly to me,
Hear me when I call.
May my prayer be set before you like incense,
May the lifting up of my hands be like the evening sacrifice.

Two years after his death Francis was pronounced a saint by Pope Gregory IX. Eventually he became the patron saint of Italy. He is also believed to be the protector of animals. In the Middle Ages, churches often held ceremonies for the blessing of animals on October 4, the feast day of St. Francis.

Before he died Francis said, "Bury me with the robbers and criminals in the place of execution." He valued every human being above himself, and did not want any honor or distinction in death. His followers, however, did not obey him. Within four years a magnificent cathedral was built in Assisi, and it was there where St. Francis was laid to rest.

MARCO POLO
1254 – 1324

Marco Polo was a merchant from the Italian city of Venice. They called him the **Prince of Travelers**. His father Niccolo was a wealthy Venetian businessman who lived in a palace on one of the canals of Venice. Niccolo often went on trading journeys to distant lands. One day Niccolo left for Asia and was away for 15 years. After he left, his wife gave birth to their son, and named him Marco. By the time Niccolo returned from his trip, his wife had died, and Marco was 15 years old.

In 1271, when Marco was 17 years old, his father and his uncle took him on a journey through Palestine, Persia, and on, all the way to China, along the **Silk Road**. The **Silk Road** was a route between Europe and Asia famous for its silk trade. Traveling along the Silk Road, caravans brought to Europe rare silks, perfumes, and spices from Persia, India, China, and Japan. The Polos first sailed, and then rode camels across mountains and deserts. In China Marco Polo's father was welcomed by Kublai Khan, the ruler of the Mongolian Golden Horde empire. The Mongols had conquered China, and Kublai Khan had declared himself Emperor of China. He liked the Polos' stories about the customs and manners of Europeans, and enjoyed the company of travelers from faraway lands.

Kublai Khan

Marco Polo lived at the court of Kublai Khan for many years and learned to speak Chinese. When Marco was 21 Kublai Khan sent him as a messenger to India and Burma. Over the years he traveled on many diplomatic missions throughout Kublai Khan's empire, visiting present-day Indonesia, Sri Lanka, and Vietnam. When Kublai Khan's daughter became engaged to the King of Persia, the Polos traveled with her from China to Persia, stopping at Borneo, Sumatra, Ceylon, and other places rarely visited by Europeans at that time. The journey was so dangerous that only 117 of the 700 travelers survived.

"Marco Polo meets Kublai Khan" by Tancredi Scarpelli

Meanwhile, in Venice, Marco's family thought the travelers were long dead. They had been away for 24 years and nobody expected them to ever come back. One day, however, in 1295, three strangers stepped off a ship in the harbor of Venice, and walked across the square of St. Mark. They wore Mongolian clothes and spoke to each other in Chinese! Their own family could hardly recognize them. Marco was 40 years old at that time. He knocked on the door of their palace. An old servant leaned out the window and asked, "Who are you and what do you want?" "We are the masters of this house," said Marco. The servant laughed and slammed the window shut. The travelers had to spend a night at an inn!

To convince Venetians that they were indeed the real Polo family, the travelers invited their family and old friends to a grand dinner. At dinner, Marco Polo wore the richest silks anyone ever saw in Venice, and rare jewels sparkled on his fingers and on the buckles of his shoes. During the dinner Marco promised to show his guests something amazing. He brought out the simple Mongolian coats which the travelers had worn when they reached Venice. Cutting open the seams, he took from inside the coat lining bags filled with rubies, emeralds, and diamonds. Every seam was ripped open and revealed its treasures, until there was a dazzling heap of jewels on the table. The jewels were so precious, even the most wealthy Venetians were stunned.

For weeks and months, friends and neighbors kept gathering to listen to Marco's stories of adventures in faraway lands. "It took us nearly four years to reach the land of China," – that's how Marco would usually start. "We went through Palestine and Arabia, Persia and Turkestan, narrowly escaping from bandits and wild beasts." "And what are the Chinese like?" asked the Venetians. "They are quiet, busy, civilized people," responded Marco. "They wear their hair in a long braid down the back, they wear odd cloth shoes, and hats with broad brims and a pointy top."

In the MIddle Ages, Venice was the most wealthy and powerful city in Europe. It had merchant ships, and it had warships to protect its trade routes from pirates. Along its canals stood marble palaces, its markets were full of traders from all over the world, and its warehouses were packed with goods from the East. It was a city state, and at the time Marco Polo returned from China, Venice was at war with another Italian city state, Genoa.

"Venice" by Luca Carlevaris

Marco Polo joined the Venetian navy, but the Venetians were defeated. Along with many of his countrymen Marco Polo was captured by the enemy and thrown into prison in Genoa. One of his fellow prisoners was skilled at writing, and Marco dictated to him an account of his travels in the East. The book was smuggled out of prison and soon the whole of Genoa was reading it. When the citizens of Genoa learned that the famous Marco Polo was in their prison, he was immediately set free.

Marco Polo's book **The Travels of Marco Polo**, has a lot of fascinating facts about the geography and culture of the ancient world. For example: "You must know that Kublai Khan keeps a lot of white horses. In fact more than 10,000 of them, and all pure white without a speck. The milk of these horses is drunk by himself and his family, and by none else." Some passages in Marco's book sound very mysterious: "There are certain crafty enchanters and astrologers at the court of Kublai Khan, who are so good at black magic that they are able to prevent any cloud or storm from passing over the spot on which the Khan's Palace stands...Whatever these magicians do is by the help of the devil, but they make people believe that it is done through the help of God...Now when the Khan desires to drink, these magicians cause the cups to move from their table – without being touched by anybody – to the table of the Khan! It's the truth and not a lie!"

Here is another passage from Marco Polo's book, typical of medieval travel reports.
"You must know that the island of Madagascar lies so far south that ships cannot go further south or visit other islands in that direction because of the strong ocean currents. It is said that in those other islands to the south is found the Gryphon bird. It is like an eagle, but one indeed of enormous size. It is so strong that it will grab an elephant and carry it high into the air, and then drop it so that it is smashed to pieces. Having so killed the elephant, the Gryphon bird swoops down on it and eats it. The people of those islands call the bird Ruc, but I couldn't tell if this be the real Gryphon, or some other bird as great. The Great Khan sent men to those parts to enquire about these curious matters. His ambassadors brought back to the Great Khan a feather of the Ruc."

Marco Polo was released from prison in 1299 and returned to Venice where his father and uncle had bought a new grand palace. Marco joined them in trading and was very successful. He got married and had 3 daughters. They say that the last words of Marco Polo before he died were: "I did not write in my book half of what I saw, for I knew I would not be believed." About 175 years after the book was written, the famous Italian from Genoa, Christopher Columbus, was inspired by Marco Polo's adventures to take a voyage across the Atlantic that led to the European discovery of America.

They say that Marco Polo brought a compass home from China. Before compasses, travelers found their way by the stars and planets. The first magnetic compass was invented in China around the 1st century AD. It was a piece of an iron-rich mineral called a *lodestone*. Lodestones are naturally magnetic. If you hang a piece of lodestone, or float it on water on a piece of wood so it can turn, it will point along the North-South direction. The English word *lodestone* means *leading stone* in Old English. At first, magnetic compasses were filled with water, but around the time Marco Polo came back to Venice, *dry* compasses started appearing in Europe. A *dry* compass was an iron needle magnetized by rubbing it with a lodestone. Compasses made travel safer and opened up a new era of exploration and worldwide travel.

A page from Marco Polo's Travels: The Polos leave Venice

DANTE ALIGHIERI

1265 – 1321

"Dante" by Sandro Botticelli

Dante Alighieri was an Italian poet of the Middle Ages, best known for his epic poem **The Divine Comedy**. Dante was born in the city-state of Florence, also called the Republic of Florence. Florence was torn between two political parties – the party that supported the Pope and the party that supported the Holy Roman Emperor. Dante's family supported the Pope. The supporters of the two parties often clashed in military conflicts. Dante fought in some of these battles.

Finally, Dante's party, the party that supported the Pope, won, but it immediately split into two new parties – the *white* party that wanted to be more independent from Rome and the Pope, and the *black* party that wanted the Pope to have the final say on all the affairs of Florence. Dante's family supported the *white* party. The *white* party seized power in Florence and sent the supporters of the *black* party into exile. When Pope Boniface VIII heard of this, he threatened to invade Florence. In 1301 Florence sent a delegation to Rome that included Dante. The Pope liked Dante and asked him to stay in Rome after the Florentine delegation left. While the *white* party delegation was in Rome, the *black* party revolted, destroyed most of Florence, and killed many *white* party supporters. Dante, who remained in Rome, was sentenced to exile and couldn't return home. All his property in Florence was seized by his enemies. Not only was Dante banished from Florence, but if caught he was to be burned alive. Later the government of Florence suggested that Dante should apologize, pay a fine, and return home. "If I cannot return without calling myself guilty, I will never return," answered Dante. In June 2008, nearly seven centuries after Dante's death, the city council of Florence officially canceled Dante's sentence!

In exile, Dante wandered from place to place, always hoping one day to return to Florence. Around 1308, he started writing his **Divine Comedy**. It took him 12 years to finish it, and he said that it was written with "his heart's blood." In the Middle Ages the word *comedy* was used for any story that started with sad and dramatic events, but had a good ending. The stories that started well but ended with death and destruction were called *tragedies*.

The Divine Comedy is the story of Dante's journey through the afterlife – the world of the dead. The afterlife, as described in the medieval teachings of the Catholic Church, consisted of Hell, Purgatory, and Heaven (or Paradise). Hell was a place for people who committed crimes and never repented. To **repent** is to be sorry for your wrongdoings. Purgatory was a place between Hell and Heaven where people who repented and prayed for forgiveness had a chance to redeem themselves despite their wrongdoings. Heaven was a place for people who had lived a holy life, or had their sins redeemed and forgiven. **The Divine Comedy** opens with these famous lines:

When I had journeyed half of my life's way,

I found myself within a shadowy forest,

for I had lost the path that does not stray.

In this shadowy world of the dead Dante has two guides. One is the Roman poet Virgil who takes Dante on a tour of Hell and Purgatory. The other is Beatrice. As a teenager, Dante fell in love with a girl named Beatrice. He had known her since he was 9. But Beatrice died young, and Dante married a woman named Gemma. However, he never forgot Beatrice. She appears as an angel in **The Divine Comedy**, and guides Dante through Paradise.

"Dante sees Beatrice" by Henry Holiday

Dante and Virgil pass through the gates of Hell.
Over the gates they see this famous inscription:

**THROUGH ME THE WAY INTO THE SUFFERING CITY,
THROUGH ME THE WAY TO THE ETERNAL PAIN,
THROUGH ME THE WAY THAT RUNS AMONG THE LOST...
ABANDON EVERY HOPE, YOU WHO ENTER HERE.**

Inside they hear the screams of the Uncommitted.
The Uncommitted are the selfish and cowardly people who took no sides in life, who didn't oppose evil and allowed it to harm others.

Here sighs, complaints, and loud cries
were echoing across the starless air...
Strange stories, horrible curses,
sounds of anger, words of suffering,
and voices shrill and faint, and beating hands..

"At the gates of Hell" by Raphael Flores

Hell is divided into 9 circles, going deeper and deeper, with the worst crimes punished at the very bottom, in the 9th circle, where Satan, the king of evil, is imprisoned. In each circle the sinners are punished in a way that reflects their sins. In Hell Dante portrays himself meeting heroes of ancient history and mythology, and many historical figures of Dante's own age, including his enemies from Florence. Dante's enemies are, of course, severely punished in Hell for their crimes! Virgil says to Dante:

How many up above consider themselves
great kings, who'll end up here like pigs in slime,
leaving behind foul memories of their crimes!

The First Circle of Hell is called **Limbo**. It's the eternal home of people who died without baptism, including people of the ancient world, like Virgil. In Limbo people are not punished, but they live far away from God.

"Descent into Hell" by Gustav Dore

In the Second Circle of Hell Dante finds people who lived their lives without self control, who ruined their marriages and betrayed those who loved them. In Hell these people are tossed around by endless storms, without rest, just as they were tossed by their selfish ideas and desires during their lifetime.

In the Third Circle Dante finds *gluttons* – people who had no control over their appetite, who wasted their lives chasing fancy food, drink, and luxury. These people are punished with a never-ending bad-smelling icy rain.

"The Seventh Circle of Hell" by Gustav Dore

The Fourth Circle is for those who valued money and possessions above everything else. For their greed they are punished by having to roll heavy weights without stopping.

In the Fifth Circle of Hell Dante meets people who had no control over their anger. They are punished by being forced to fight each other in a slimy marsh. Those whose anger was quiet and didn't cause fights are lying under the surface of the black slimy water.

In the Sixth Circle of Hell we find *heretics* – people whose ideas are contrary to Christian teachings. In this circle Dante placed atheists – non-believers who teach that there is no life after death. As punishment, heretics are trapped in burning tombs.

The Seventh Circle of Hell is occupied by people guilty of violent crimes – crimes against human life and against God's creations. Murderers and tyrants are endlessly drowning in a river of boiling blood and fire. People who committed *suicide* – killed themselves – are turned into trees, on which *harpies* – birds with the faces of women – feed.

"The Seventh Circle of Hell" by Gustav Dore

People guilty of blasphemy – being disrespectful toward God – are running in circles on burning sand under a rain of flames.

The Eighth Circle of Hell punishes the crimes of fraud and deception. Virgil explains to Dante:

Of every evil that earns hate in Heaven,
injustice is the worst; and each such crime
by force or fraud brings harm to other men.
Fraud is a crime peculiar to men,
God finds it more destructive – and therefore,
deceivers are the worst and suffer more.

Among the sinners are **panderers**, who used people's fears or hopes to make them serve the panderers' selfish goals. They are being whipped by demons. There, too, are the *flatterers*, who used flattery to gain the trust of others and then deceived them. The flatterers are drowning in toilet waste. There are also found

"The Ninth Circle of Hell" by Gustav Courtois
Left: "Hell" by Gustav Dore

the fortune-tellers. As punishment their heads are twisted backwards so they can no longer see what's ahead, because they deceived people by pretending to see into the future. Corrupt politicians are being cooked in a lake of boiling pitch. Hypocrites – **pretenders** – wear clothes that are gold on the outside, but inside they are made of lead, and their weight is crushing. Thieves are being eaten alive by snakes. **Sowers of discord** – rulers and religious leaders who caused wars – are being slashed into pieces by sword.

In the Ninth and final circle of Hell, Dante and Virgil find traitors. They are frozen forever in a lake of ice.

Purgatory in Dante's *Divine Comedy* is a mountain that has 7 terraces or levels of suffering and spiritual growth. On each level the souls of sinners learn from their mistakes. The proud carry huge stones on their backs. The eyes of the envious are sewn shut. Those who spent their life quarrelling wander in clouds of suffocating smoke.

Heaven, or Paradise, consists of 9 celestial spheres. In the first seven spheres Dante meets the souls of saints, historical figures, and common people who lived righteous lives. The Eighth Sphere is the sphere of Faith, Hope, and Love. Here Dante and Beatrice meet Mary, mother of Jesus, the Apostles Peter and John who question Dante whether he has faith, hope, and love. The Ninth Sphere is the home of angels. Beyond the Ninth Sphere is the spiritual world. Here, God's love is symbolically represented as a beautiful rose. Souls that rise to Heaven live on the petals of this rose. Finally Dante sees God who is shown as three circles – the Trinity.

"The envious in Purgatory" by Tancredi Scarpelli

"Dante meets Beatrice in Heaven"
by Carl Wilhelm Friedrich Oesterly
Right: "Heaven" by Gustav Dore

FRA ANGELICO
1395 – 1455

Fra Angelico's birth name was Guido di Pietro. He was born in the Italian province of Tuscany. When he was 20 he decided to become a monk of the Dominican Order. At that time he was already a painter. When a person becomes a monk or a nun they receive a new name. Guido's new name was Giovanni. Fra Angelico means *angelic friar* in Italian. It was a nickname he received for the holiness of his life. 16th-century Italian author Georgio Vasari wrote in his book **Lives of the Most Eminent Painters, Sculptors, and Architects,** that "Fra Giovanni never took a brush or pencil in his hand without a prayer."

"Angels visit Fra Angelico" by Paul-Hippolyte Flandrin

Right: "Anunciation" – Archangel Gabriel visits Mary, mother of Jesus – fresco by Fra Angelico

Fra Angelico became well-known by painting *frescoes* of scenes from the life of Jesus on the walls of churches and monasteries. A *fresco* is a painting done in watercolor on wet plaster – a white material used to cover walls and ceilings. The word comes from the Italian *al fresco – on the fresh* (plaster). In the Middle Ages in Europe, most people couldn't read or write. Church services were in Latin, but Latin had not been an everyday spoken language since the fall of the Roman Empire, so the common people could not understand church services. To help people learn, churches hired artists to paint frescoes that told Bible stories and explained the main ideas of the Christian faith on the church walls.

Fra Angelico also illustrated books. Medieval books were *manuscripts* copied by hand. The word *manuscript* comes from the Latin *manu – by hand* and *scriptus – written*. Manuscripts were *illuminated*, which means *illustrated*, by artists. Illustrations couldn't be easily copied, so illustrated books were rare and precious. Illuminators used a lot of gold paint and expensive pigments. For example, blue paint was made from powdered semi-precious stone *lapis lazuli*. Fra Angelico illustrated prayer books, books of church music, and copies of the Bible. There is a medieval legend about a monk painter who was illustrating a page of a manuscript when he was called away to do some service for the poor. He went unwillingly because he wanted to finish his painting. But when he returned, he found his work had been finished by an angel. People who knew Fra Angelico told similar stories about him.

Along with frescoes and book illustrations Fra Angelico also created *icons* – paintings done mostly on wood, displayed in church or in private homes, and considered sacred. Often a *patron* – such as a wealthy merchant or a church official – *commissioned* such paintings to an artist. To *commission* a work of art is to instruct an artist to create it, and to pay for the artist's work. On many paintings in medieval churches artists included portraits of their patrons. Patrons liked a lot of gold in the icons they commissioned. The painting was viewed as a statement about the patron. The more gold, the wealthier was the patron!

"Coronation of Mary, mother of Jesus"
- an icon by Fra Angelico

Soon the fame of Fra Angelico spread outside the monastery walls, and reached the ears of Cosimo Medici, one of the most powerful citizens of the Italian city of Florence. Medici offered the monks of Fra Angelico's monastery the opportunity to move to Florence and, when they were settled in the Convent of San Marco in Florence, he invited Fra Angelico to paint frescoes on the walls.

Soon the Pope himself invited Fra Angelico to Rome to paint the walls of a chapel there. When the Pope saw Fra Angelico's work, he said to him: "A man who can paint such pictures, can do well whatever he undertakes. Would you like to become the Archbishop of Florence?"

The position of an archbishop would have given Fra Angelico power and wealth, but he refused. "He might have been rich," writes Vasari, "but to him being rich was being satisfied with little. He might have ruled many, but he would not, saying that it was less tiresome to obey others. He was offered many honors, but he despised them, saying that the only honor he wanted was to avoid Hell and be closer to Heaven."

In 1982 the Catholic Church proclaimed Fra Angelico a saint and the patron of artists.

His *epitaph* – the words written on his grave – reads:

The deeds that count on Earth are not the ones that count in Heaven.
I, Giovanni, am the flower of Tuscany.

"Mary and baby Jesus" – an icon by Fra Angelico

JOAN OF ARC
1412 – 1431

Joan of Arc, or **Jeanne d'Arc** in French, was born in the little village of Domrémy in Eastern France. Her father, Jacques d'Arc, who was a farmer, often talked to her about the political situation in France. France was in the middle of the so-called **Hundred Years' War** with England. At that point England was winning. The English occupied most of France, including Paris. The King of France had died and his son, Prince Charles, was supposed to become king, but he did not dare to be crowned. The French were good soldiers, but they needed a real leader. Prince Charles held his court in his castle at the little town of Chinon in southern France. Instead of planning battles, he entertained himself with music performances and knights' tournaments. Meanwhile, the land was in a terrible state. Peasants had no courage to plant their crops, because armies kept trampling down their fields. Merchants closed their trade for fear of being robbed on the roads.

When Joan of Arc was 13 she began to have visions of angels. In a vision she had in her garden, Archangel Michael appeared to her and told her, "Joan, you can save France from the English. Go and help Prince Charles. You will lead the French soldiers into battle, you will win, and Charles will be crowned king in the city of Rheims." Rheims was the place where all French kings had been crowned. The vision was so beautiful, Joan cried. When she was 16 she decided to take action. "I have been chosen by God to fulfill his purpose," she said to her family, and prepared to leave her home.
Her parents, friends, the village priest, all tried to stop her, but it was in vain. "I will do the work God has laid out for me," she insisted. Little by little, people began to believe her and stopped trying to discourage her.
Joan went to the local town and asked the commander of the town garrison to take her to see Prince Charles. He just laughed at her. But Joan did not give up. She soon returned, and predicted the outcome of one of the battles days before the messengers arrived with the report about it.

A fragment of a medieval crown, France, 13th century

The garrison commander was impressed, and agreed to take her to Chinon where Charles lived. It was unusual for a girl to travel without her parents. To protect herself from the curiosity of strangers, Joan cut her hair short, and dressed in men's clothes.

Prince Charles heard that Joan believed she had a mission from God, and decided to test her. He dressed as a French knight, and when she arrived he stood among his knights, thinking that she wouldn't recognize him. Joan, however, walked up straight to him and fell down on her knees before him. "God give you good life, my king," she said.
"I am not the king," said Prince Charles, still testing her.
"You will be king," replied Joan. "I am sent by the King of Heaven to tell you that you will go to Rheims and will be crowned King of France."
Charles was amazed. He listened as she explained to him that God had ordered her to lead French soldiers into battle. When Joan was asked why she needed an army if God wished to save the French people, she responded, "God helps those who help themselves."

While in Chinon, Joan saw soldiers leaving for the French city of Orléans, at that time besieged by the English. She said that if she led the army, she would lift the siege of Orléans. The English had begun the siege of Orléans in October of 1428. They had taken towns around Orléans and built a chain of forts that surrounded the city. Orléans was the "key to the south of France." The French knew that if Orléans was lost, all of France was lost.

Prince Charles' advisors told him that if God was on his side, Joan would, indeed, stop the siege of Orléans. So Charles let Joan go to Orléans with the soldiers who were carrying supplies for the city. In April of 1429, Joan left Chinon. She was 18. She wore white armor and rode a black war-horse. In one hand she carried an ancient sword that she had found near the tomb of a saint, and in the other a banner.

"Joan of Arc" by Jules Eugène Lenepveu

Her banner was pure white, and on it was embroidered a picture of two angels carrying lily flowers, and an image of God holding up the world. Lily flowers – *fleurs-de-lis*, in French – were the symbol of both France and Catholic saints, and appeared in many medieval *coat of arms* emblems.

Joan entered Orléans, where people greeted her with cheering and celebrations. They had heard ancient legends saying that a girl dressed in armor would save France. French soldiers were inspired by Joan's courage and faith. She declared that the war against the English was just and holy, because they had invaded France against the will of God. Joan led the troops of Prince Charles into battle, and the French started winning! Most decisions were still taken by Charles' military commanders, but Joan rode into battle at the head of the French army, holding her white banner. She later stated that she didn't use the sword and never killed anyone.

fleur-de-lis

"Joan of Arc in battle" by Frank Craig

"Coronation of Charles VII" by Jules-Eugene Lenepveu

Joan wrote a few letters addressed to the English soldiers and their commanders. Here is one of Joan's letters tied to an arrow and shot by the French into one of the English forts: "You, men of England, who have no right in the Kingdom of France, the King of Heaven orders and notifies you through me, Joan, to leave your fortresses and go back to your own country, or I will produce a clash of arms to be eternally remembered. And this is the third and last time I have written to you; I shall not write anything further."

The Siege of Orléans became a turning point in the Hundred Years' War between France and England. The lifting of the siege was the first big French victory. At some point Joan was wounded by an arrow in her shoulder, and left the battle. Her soldiers immediately began to retreat. But Joan told them: "Watch my banner! When it touches the walls of the fort, you shall enter it." She mounted her horse, rode to the wall of the fort, touched it with her banner, and the fort was taken. The enemy troops fled and the siege of Orléans was over. Joan's fame spread throughout France and England.

The French thought the victory at Orléans was a sign from God. The English did not agree that God was on the side of the French. Joan was sent by the devil, they said, and Joan defeated them only through the use of black magic. However, like most Europeans in medieval times, Joan thought that any act of magic was against God. When she was wounded, French soldiers offered to put what they believed was a magic charm on her wound. But she refused, saying, "I would rather die than do a thing which I know to be against the will of God."

Charles traveled to Rheims and was crowned King of France in the beautiful Rheims cathedral. Joan stood by his side, her banner in her hand. Charles was anointed with holy oil by the archbishop, and then, as the crown was put on his head, trumpets rang out, announcing to the waiting crowds that France had, again, a king. All the people cried "Long live King Charles!" Joan hoped to return home to her parents, but King Charles asked her to stay until France was completely freed from the English. His soldiers had come to believe that they would win a victory wherever Joan led them.

There were rumors that during the battles fire was seen flashing around her banner. Many believed that Joan was a saint, and asked to kiss her hand or her armor. But Joan told them,
"I work no miracles. I am nothing but the instrument God uses to help France."

As Joan continued leading the French troops, she was captured by the Duke of Burgundy, one of the king's enemies. For a large sum of money the duke gave Joan into the hands of the English. The English threw her in prison in Rouen. She tried to escape a few times, and the French troops made a couple attempts to save her, but they failed. After a year, Joan was accused of being a witch, and brought to trial.

At the trial Joan's enemies focused on the fact that Joan had dressed as a man when traveling or leading soldiers in battle. In the Middle Ages people believed that only witches and sorcerers *cross-dressed*, that is dressed as the opposite gender. Joan was sentenced to being burned alive, and perished.

25 years later the Catholic Church declared the accusations against Joan false, and in 1920 she was canonized as a saint.

Above: "Capture of Joan of Arc" by Adolphe Dillens
"Joan of Arc interrogation" by Paul Delaroche

JOHANNES GUTENBERG

1400 – 1468

Johannes Gutenberg was the inventor of the printing press who introduced book printing in Europe. Gutenberg was born in Mainz, Germany. Very likely, as a boy, he was taught to read, but the books from which he learned were not printed books, like ours today. They were manuscripts copied by hand, letter by letter. Since the times of ancient Egypt, Greece, and Rome, people had used sharply pointed instruments to write on wooden tablets covered with wax, or dried goat skins, or tree bark, or sheets made from the papyrus plant. They wrote on one side and rolled it up – those were the ancient *scrolls*. Scrolls were kept in jars or wooden boxes. Then, Ancient Romans invented the *codex* – a book whose leaves were bound into a spine. In the Middle Ages manuscripts were written on *parchment*, a writing material made from the skins of sheep and goats. Both the materials and the work of *scribes* – people who copied the books – cost a lot. Only wealthy people had enough money to own books.

While Gutenberg was growing up, a new way of making books appeared – *block-printing*. For each page a printer took a block of wood, wrote on it the words he was going to print, and cut away the wood around the letters, leaving each letter raised. The letters were inked. Then they pressed paper to the wooden letters, and the printed page was ready. Using blocks, printers could make copies of a book much faster than a scribe could copy a manuscript. But making blocks took a long time, and each block printed only one page. Only one side of the paper was used, so every pair of pages had to be glued together. It was a lot of work. Such books were called *block books*. Most of them were bibles that had pictures and almost no text. They were known as *poor man's Bibles*.

A page from a block-printed bible

Gutenberg enjoyed reading. He felt it was unfair that only rich people could buy and read books. He dreamed of inventing a quick way of printing, but he didn't want his friends or neighbors to know what he was doing. In Strasburg where he lived, there was a ruined old monastery building. Gutenberg rented one room in that building, repaired it, and used it as his workshop. He left home early in the morning and came back late at night. His neighbors wondered what was going on. There were rumors that he had secret meetings with the devil! Gutenberg did not care much what people thought. He kept experimenting with making letters to print books.

At last the time came when he had no money left. He went back home to Mainz, and there he met a rich goldsmith named Faust. Gutenberg told him about his ideas, and Faust gave him the money he needed. Soon Gutenberg came up with a breakthrough idea. He started making little wooden blocks with a single letter at one end. He could make words from these blocks. While the old wood blocks had a whole page carved on one block and couldn't be reused, these new blocks were movable: They could be repositioned and reused to make different pages. He could set them up to print one page, then take them apart and set them up again to print a different page!

Wooden type blocks did not always print the letters clearly, so Gutenberg started experimenting with metal letter blocks. He invented a way to connect them together in special forms, and made a printing press. In 1455 Gutenberg printed his first book. It was a Latin Bible. Today we call it the **Gutenberg Bible**. About 180 copies were printed –— some on paper and some on parchment. Paper was first invented in the 2nd century AD in China, and by the 13th century the first paper mills started appearing in Europe. It took Gutenberg a long time before he succeeded, and Faust lost patience. He wanted his money back. Faust went to court, and the judge ordered Gutenberg to give everything he owned, including the tools he used, and the bibles he printed to Faust as payment of his debt. Faust took over Gutenberg's printing press and made printing his business.

Movable metal type

This was devastating for Gutenberg, but he didn't lose his courage. He continued building printing presses and working to improve the technique of book printing. Gutenberg's great invention didn't bring him fame. It was long after he died when people started talking about him as the inventor of book printing. However, thanks to him, book printing spread all over Europe, and soon printing presses were at work in most big cities. Bibles and other books were sold so cheaply that almost anyone could now afford to buy books. Christopher Columbus, who was born 4 years before the Gutenberg Bible was printed, had a geography book bought for him by his father. It was printed with Gutenberg's movable type!

Historians consider Gutenberg's invention of the printing press the end of the Middle Ages and the beginning of the modern period of human history. As books became less expensive, education and science started growing, news and ideas started spreading much faster, and that opened the doors to the next era of history – the **Renaissance**, or **rebirth** of the ancient traditions of philosophy, education, and science – formed in ancient Greece and Rome, and forgotten in Europe during the Dark Ages.

Medieval castle, Germany, and a page from the Gutenberg Bible with hand-painted decorations.

www.ingramcontent.com/pod-product-compliance
Lightning Source LLC
Chambersburg PA
CBHW041433010526
44118CB00002B/61